THE BOYS ARE BACK

DAK, ZEKE, AND A NEW COWBOYS ERA IN BIG D

JEAN-JACQUES TAYLOR

TRIUMPH
BOOKS

This book is available in quantity at special discounts for your group or organization.
For further information contact:

Triumph Books LLC
814 North Franklin Street
Chicago, Illinois, 60610
Phone: (312) 337-0747
www.triumphbooks.com

Printed in the United States of America

ISBN: 978-1-62937-519-9

Content packaged by Alex Lubertozzi

All photos courtesy of AP Images

Contents

Cowboys vs. Seahawks

The Preseason Game That Changed the Franchise

Tony Romo, fueled by a competitive spirit that's been a part of his soul since the first time he held a ball in his arms, made a decision in the Dallas Cowboys' third preseason game based on instinct instead of common sense.

It was a decision that changed his career and altered the direction of the Cowboys' franchise.

Romo, trying to elude the Seattle Seahawks' pass rush on the game's third play, slid left and took off from the pocket. As he crossed the line of scrimmage, Romo began to slide when 260-pound defensive end Cliff Avril tackled Romo from behind. He landed atop Romo, scrunching him into the turf at CenturyLink Field, with 13:27 left in the first quarter. As Romo lay prone on the turf reaching for his back, the Cowboys found their season in flux.

Again.

Remember, Romo broke his collarbone twice during the 2015 season, and the Cowboys finished 4–12 as the veteran missed all or parts of 14 games. Romo broke his collarbone in Week 2 against the Philadelphia Eagles. He missed seven games, returning in Week 10 against Miami, leading the Cowboys to a 24–14 win over the Dolphins. But four days later, he broke his collarbone again on the final play of the third quarter of a Thanksgiving Day debacle against the Carolina Panthers.

Brandon Weeden, signed to be the backup in 2015, and Matt Cassel, acquired in a trade with the Buffalo Bills the week after Romo suffered the injury, combined to go 1–9 as starters. They passed for a total of 2,014 yards with seven touchdowns and nine interceptions. Their shoddy performance is the reason why the Cowboys drafted Dak Prescott in the fourth round of the 2016 draft.

Prescott became the backup when Kellen Moore broke his right fibula on the fourth day of training camp. The Cowboys didn't want to expose Romo to any undue risk, so they didn't use him in the first two preseason games. Coach Jason Garrett planned to use Romo for a half, then sit him down until the regular season.

Romo's impulsive decision ruined that plan and made Prescott the focal point of the Cowboys' offense. If he couldn't handle it, the Cowboys would have to acquire another quarterback. Maybe they'd spend a late-round pick on the Kansas City Chiefs' Nick Foles or the Cleveland Browns' Josh McCown. Either way, they'd be asking another marginal quarterback to learn

Cowboys quarterback Tony Romo lies on the turf in pain (above right) after getting tackled by Seahawks defensive end Cliff Avril during the first quarter of Dallas' third preseason game of 2016. Romo is examined by trainer Jim Maurer (right) after Romo injured his back on the play.

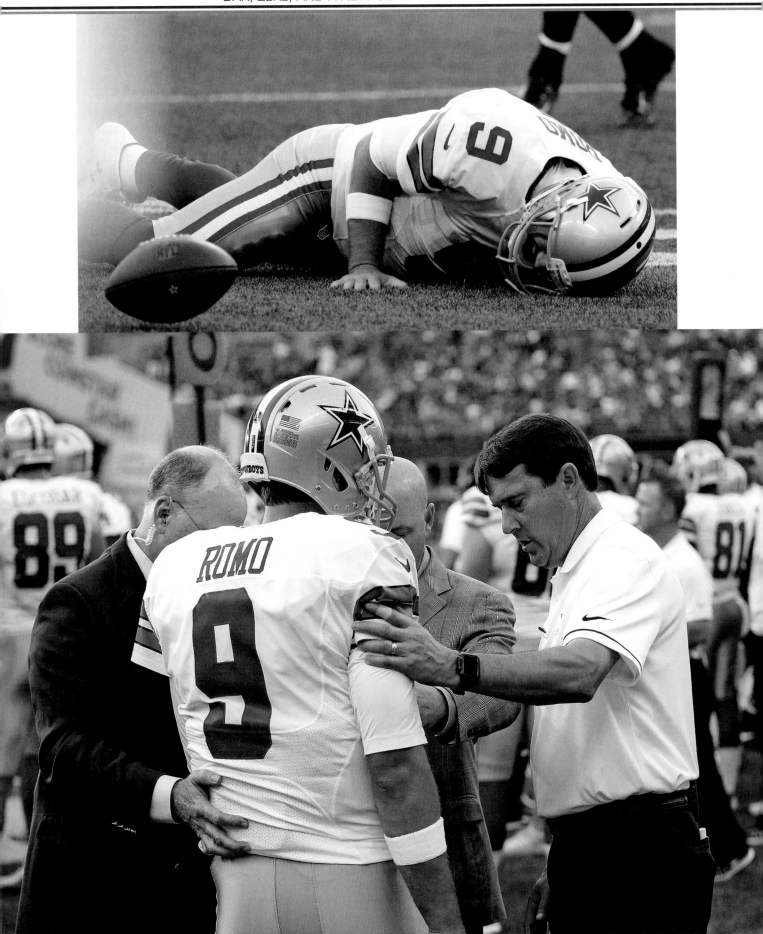

the offense and be productive in a short time. That approach didn't work in 2015, and the Cowboys didn't want to go that route again.

Prescott's performance against Seattle was a harbinger. He completed 17 of 23 passes for 116 yards and a touchdown. He finished Romo's drive and then led the Cowboys on a seven-play, 81-yard drive, culminating with a 17-yard touchdown pass to tight end Jason Witten. Prescott's touchdown pass demonstrated the confidence he had in his arm, his accuracy, and his tight end, who was covered tightly by a linebacker. The pass zoomed right past a defender's ear—he was looking at Witten, not the ball—and Witten snagged it for the score.

While Prescott was leading a scoring drive against one of the NFL's best defenses—Seattle played 10 of its 11 Week 1 starters—Romo lobbied Garrett and the training staff to get back in the game. He walked off the field under his own power and tossed passes on the sideline to see if he felt discomfort throwing. Garrett denied Romo's requests.

"That was a perfectly timed situation. I was going into the slide, and he obviously caught me from behind," Romo said after the game. "In a weird way, I feel good about the fact that was probably as tough of a hit I took on the back as I've had in the last five years. In that regard, I feel very lucky that it could hold up and keep going."

Cowboys rookie backup quarterback Dak Prescott (No. 4) came into the preseason game versus Seattle after Romo went down and completed 17 of 23 passes for 116 yards and a touchdown to tight end Jason Witten.

Against the Seahawks, Elliott gave the Cowboys a glimpse of the future.

Ezekiel Elliott also made his debut against Seattle, a few hours after he visited Herban Legends, a marijuana dispensary a few blocks from the Cowboys' downtown hotel. It was Elliott's first introduction to what it means to be a member of America's Team. It's legal to sell marijuana in Washington, so there was nothing illegal about his visit. That said, using marijuana would violate the NFL's substance-abuse policy and could eventually lead to a suspension.

While his judgment before the game was questionable, his performance during the game was beyond reproach. Elliott, the fourth player taken in the 2016 draft, missed the first two preseason games with a slight hamstring strain. He would've played had they been regular-season games, but the key to the Cowboys' season was making sure he was ready to play when the season began. The Cowboys drafted Elliott even though Darren McFadden rushed for 1,089 yards, fourth in the NFL. But McFadden is not a difference-maker, which is what the Cowboys wanted. In 2014 DeMarco Murray rushed for a league-leading 1,845 yards on 392 carries as the Cowboys finished 12–4 and won the NFC East.

Murray signed a five-year, $42 million contract with the Philadelphia Eagles as a free agent after 2014. The Cowboys drafted Elliott because he was the key to establishing their offensive identity, even though they needed help on a defense that allowed 23.4 points and 347.9 yards per game.

Against the Seahawks, Elliott gave the Cowboys a glimpse of the future.

On the Cowboys' second series, Elliott gained a yard off right tackle. Then he zoomed around right end for nine yards before scooting out of bounds for a first down. He gained another nine yards on his third consecutive carry, following All-Pro guard Zack Martin around right end and running through star linebacker Bobby Wagner at the end of the run. On Elliott's fourth consecutive carry, he headed right again, cut upfield, and ran through safety Kam Chancellor, among the game's hardest-hitting safeties, for four more yards.

Message delivered. Chancellor took notice.

Prescott's short pass to Elliott in the middle of the field was knocked down at the line of scrimmage, but Chancellor delivered a big hit to Elliott's shoulder that sent him sprawling to the ground. He immediately popped up and took several steps toward Chancellor. "That let me know about him right then," Dez Bryant told ESPN.com. "Kam is one of the best in the league, and Zeke didn't care. He stepped right to him."

Two plays later, Elliott ran off left tackle, powered through an arm tackle, and collided with Chancellor at the Seattle 20. Three yards later, cornerback Richard Sherman and linebacker K.J. Wright pulled Elliott down as Chancellor picked himself up off the ground.

"He played 12 plays in that Seattle game, and I think he showed everybody the kind of player he was," Garrett said. "We never had any doubt about the kind of football player that young man is. You talk about competitors, and he's one of the great natural competitors I've ever been around."

Elliott finished the game with seven carries for 48 yards and considerably more respect from his teammates and the coaching staff than when the game began. ★

Cowboys rookie running back Ezekiel Elliott saw his first NFL action in a preseason game against the Seahawks, rushing seven times for 48 yards and impressing his teammates and opponents alike.

A Bad Break

Romo's Injury-Plagued 2015 Led to the Acquisition of Dak and Zeke

Troy Aikman spoiled Jerry Jones. It's easy to see why. Aikman, the first player taken in the 1989 draft, was selected two months after Jones bought the team. Four years after the Cowboys drafted Aikman, he led Dallas to its first Super Bowl championship since 1977. Then he led the Cowboys to another. And two years later, they added another.

Aikman led Dallas to a then unprecedented three Super Bowl wins in four seasons. That's legendary—the kind of accomplishment no Cowboys' quarterback had achieved since Roger Staubach led the Cowboys to a pair of championships in the 1970s.

Staubach's heroics—he was the starter on coach Tom Landry's two championship teams—helped transform the Cowboys from "Next Year's Champions" into Super Bowl champions. Staubach established the standard for a Cowboys quarterback, and no one came close to matching it until Aikman showed up.

As Aikman established himself as one of the NFL's best quarterbacks, Jones never even considered drafting a quarterback of the future. He signed quality veteran backups such as Steve Beuerlein, Rodney Peete, Bernie Kosar, and Wade Wilson because, if something ever happened to Aikman, the Cowboys wanted someone capable of guiding a championship-caliber team through a few games or a season.

So when Aikman abruptly retired at the end of the 2000 season, Jones was caught unprepared to replace him. After all, they had drafted only two quarterbacks since Aikman. Jimmy Johnson had used a first-round supplemental pick on Steve Walsh, his quarterback at the University of Miami, and the Cowboys drafted Bill Musgrave in the fourth round of the 1991 draft. Three games into the 1990 season, the Cowboys traded Walsh to New Orleans for first-, second-, and third-round draft picks. The Cowboys took right tackle Erik Williams in the third round, and the other two picks were dealt to New England as part of a package to move up and select defensive tackle Russell Maryland with the No. 1 pick overall. Maryland and Williams were key starters on the Cowboys' championship teams.

The lack of attention the Cowboys spent on the game's most important position caught up with them after Aikman retired. From 2000 until Tony Romo took over at halftime of a loss to the New York Giants

On September 20, 2015, Tony Romo broke his left collarbone after getting sacked by Eagles linebacker Jordan Hicks during the second game of the season in Philadelphia. He would miss the next seven games due to the injury.

in 2006, Quincy Carter, Anthony Wright, Ryan Leaf, Clint Stoerner, Chad Hutchinson, Vinny Testaverde, Drew Henson, and Drew Bledsoe all started at least one game for the Cowboys as the team went 43–59.

Romo, the Cowboys' starter for the next decade, went 78–49. The former undrafted free agent signed with Dallas instead of the Denver Broncos, who offered him $10,000 more than the Cowboys. Romo picked Dallas because he figured there was a better chance to earn a roster spot in Dallas than Denver.

Romo evolved into one of the NFL's best quarterbacks over the next decade in a career defined by incredible highs and lows. He was also among the league's most durable quarterbacks, missing only 15 games in his first nine seasons—and 10 of those occurred in 2010, when he suffered a broken collarbone.

In 2013 he missed the Week 17 win-and-get-in game against Philadelphia with a ruptured disc in his back that required off-season surgery. In 2014 he missed a November 2 game against the Arizona

Cardinals after he was kneed in the back a week earlier against Washington. In 2015 Romo broke his collarbone in the second game of the season when Philadelphia linebacker Jordan Hicks sacked him in the third quarter. The Cowboys beat Philadelphia but lost its next seven games with Brandon Weeden and Matt Cassel as their starting quarterbacks.

Romo hurried back, knowing he could break the collarbone again. He lasted seven quarters.

After leading the Cowboys to a 24–14 road win over the Miami Dolphins, Romo fractured his collarbone again when he was sacked on the last play of the third quarter of the Carolina Panthers' 33–14 win. He missed the rest of the regular season, and had off-season surgery to repair the injury. The Cowboys went 1–11 with any quarterback not named Romo, prompting Jones and coach Jason Garrett to make drafting a quarterback a priority in the off-season.

Since drafting Carter in 2002, Texas A&M's Stephen McGee was the only quarterback the Cowboys had drafted. Jones had tried to use out-of-the-box

Cowboys backup QB Brandon Weeden (No. 3) gets pressured by New Orleans safety Kenny Vaccaro during the Cowboys 26–20 overtime loss to the Saints on October 4, 2015, the second of seven straight losses by Dallas during Romo's absence.

thinking to find quarterbacks by acquiring the rights to former baseball players such as Hutchinson and Henson, but they didn't work out. Quarterbacks taken in the first round had such a high bust rate, Jones figured it was better to spend a few million instead of the long-term, eight-digit contracts it would cost to secure a quarterback at the top of the draft.

Since Jerry Jones bought the team in 1989, the Cowboys have drafted just five quarterbacks. No team has drafted fewer—not even franchises such as Jacksonville and Carolina, which joined the NFL in 1995, or even the Houston Texans, who didn't

start playing until 2002. In that span, 22 teams have drafted at least 10 quarterbacks, including Green Bay, which has taken 17. Reality said the Cowboys would eventually need to use a premium draft to select a quarterback to find Romo's eventual successor.

The Cowboys wanted Memphis quarterback Paxton Lynch in the first round of the 2016 draft, and they were prepared to trade up to acquire him. The Cowboys offered Seattle its picks in the second (No. 34 overall) and fourth round (No. 101) for the No. 26 pick, but Denver offered Seattle a swap of first-round picks, plus a third-round pick (No. 94).

Romo grabs his left shoulder after reinjuring his collarbone against the Carolina Panthers on November 26, 2015, in his second game back after breaking his collarbone in Week 2. Panthers defensive end Mario Addison (97) looks on.

The Cowboys then tried to move up to the top of the fourth round to take Michigan State quarterback Connor Cook, but Oakland swapped fourth-round picks and gave the Browns a fifth-round pick, something the Cowboys didn't have.

The Cowboys finally took Prescott, the seventh quarterback selected in the 2016 draft. Jared Goff and Carson Wentz went 1–2 in the draft, and Lynch was the only other quarterback taken in the first round. Christian Hackenberg went to the New York Jets in the second round; Jacoby Brissett went to New England in the third round; Cody Kessler went to the Browns in the third round; and Cook went before Prescott in the fourth round.

On April 28, 2016, the Dallas Cowboys selected Ohio State University running back Ezekiel Elliott with the No. 4 overall pick in the NFL Draft.

"I ran around the house acting like I was the Cowboys' quarterback my whole life, so for it to all come true, it's such a blessing," Prescott said. "Just being here with my family, and [owner Jerry] Jones gave me that call, and just the excitement to have my family a majority of Cowboys fans, it was awesome."

He was supposed to be the third-string quarterback behind Kellen Moore, allowing him to slowly acclimate to the NFL and learn a pro-style offense since he had spent virtually all of his time at Mississippi State in the shotgun.

"A great leader, positively impacted everybody there, has played big in big games, and has done a lot of really good things on the field," Garrett said of Prescott. "Physically, he is big. He is strong. He can throw it. He can run. He is a very experienced player. Again, he is developmental from the standpoint that he is young and he has to learn how we want to do things, but there are a lot of tools there and a lot of great character qualities that you love."

Fate intervened.

Circumstance thrust Prescott into the starter's role, and he responded with 3,667 yards passing with 23 touchdowns and four interceptions, while being named Rookie of the Year. ★

Dak Prescott, a fourth-round draft pick, gets under center during Cowboys' rookie camp in Irving, Texas, on May 6, 2016. He was expected to be a third-string quarterback for the team before fate intervened.

Jason Garrett

The Coach Who Gave the Franchise Identity and Direction

Jason Garrett's first practice as a head coach on November 10, 2010, showed everyone in the Dallas Cowboys organization what he was all about. It began about 45 minutes earlier than Wade Phillips' practices had for the previous three-and-a-half years, and it had an edge to it. Instead of just the offensive players jogging from drill to drill, the defensive players did too.

And everybody wore full pads.

Garrett wanted his practices more physical than Phillips did. He wanted a team that controlled the line of scrimmage, and the best way to do that is to be physical in practice and develop that kind of demeanor. "Nobody sitting on the coolers, stuff like that," defensive end Stephen Bowen said in the locker room. "Just everybody alert, paying attention."

And after practice, when the players eat lunch and handle their media responsibilities, no one plays cards. Nobody slams dominoes either. "The locker room is clean, too, ain't it?" receiver Roy Williams said, laughing.

Garrett wanted to recreate the identity the Cowboys had in the 1990s, when he was a third-string quarterback and the Cowboys ruled the NFL. He wanted a physical football team built around a dominant offensive line that led an offense that could attack multiple ways. He also wanted a team mentally tough enough to win football games regardless of conditions or circumstance.

Owner Jerry Jones gave Garrett an opportunity to coach the Cowboys because Wade Phillips failed. Phillips, hired in 2007 after Bill Parcells retired after four seasons, was the complete opposite as a leader. Parcells was forever churning the bottom of the roster, putting players on a constant edge as they wondered if they had done enough on a weekly basis to earn a roster spot. Phillips created a much more familial environment. He preferred not to work out players every Tuesday, the players' off day, because he wanted to create an atmosphere where loyalty ruled. Phillips thought that made players perform harder and better for him.

Phillips' first season the Cowboys went 13–3 and won the NFC East and had home-field advantage throughout the playoffs. They lost 21–17 to the eventual Super Bowl–champion New York Giants, a team Dallas had beaten twice in the regular season—45–35 and 31–20.

The Cowboys went 9–7 in 2008, failing to compete in a 44–6 loss to Philadelphia in a

Cowboys head coach Jason Garrett during a game against the Philadelphia Eagles on October 30, 2016, in Arlington, Texas. Garrett has led Dallas since taking over mid-season in 2010 and has compiled a 58–46 record, 1–2 in the playoffs.

win-and-get-in-the-playoffs game in Week 17. Dallas regrouped and went 11–5 in 2009 with Phillips' defense posting consecutive shutouts in the final two games of the regular season.

Dallas then beat Philadelphia 34–14 in the first round of the playoffs before getting blown out 34–3 by the Minnesota Vikings the next week. Still, the Cowboys won their first playoff game since 1996 and seemed primed to make a deep playoff run in 2010.

They didn't. Actually, they didn't come close.

Phillips, doomed by Jones' never-ending obsession with marketing the Cowboys, lost control of the team in training camp, and they never recovered. The Cowboys spent the first two weeks of training camp in San Antonio, then flew to Ohio where they played in the Hall of Fame Game. The Cowboys then flew across country to Oxnard, California, about an hour north of Los Angeles, where they spent the last three weeks of training camp.

When it ended, the Cowboys had been away from their homes from July 23 through August 31. They would play like a tired team, unable to finish. Dallas started 1–5, losing each game by a touchdown or less. Romo broke his collarbone in Week 7 when rookie fullback Chris Gronkowski failed to pick up a blitzing New York Giants linebacker. Then came a 35–17 loss to Jacksonville and an embarrassing 45–7 national TV loss to the Green Bay Packers that signified the end of Phillips' tenure in Dallas.

Less than 24 hours later, Jones fired Phillips 10 months after the coach had received a two-year extension. Phillips finished his career in Dallas with a 34–22 record and a .607 winning percentage, which trails only Barry Switzer's .634 percentage in franchise history.

Jones called Phillips at 1:45 Monday afternoon for a meeting in the owner's office, where he notified him that he'd no longer be coaching the Cowboys. Forty-five minutes later, Jones summoned Garrett and told him that he was going to be the interim head coach with a chance to earn the job. About 3:00 PM Jones and Phillips met with the players. Jones talked for about 10 minutes; Phillips spoke for five in an emotional setting, as you would expect.

Then it was time for Garrett, standing at the lectern, to explain what he hoped to do with this franchise stuck in the abyss of mediocrity. "I think the personality of this group going forward will have my stamp on it a little more than it has in the past," Garrett said that day. "I've been fortunate to be in this organization at a lot of different levels—as a player, as an assistant coach, as a coordinator and now as a head coach. What we're going to try to do is restore that tradition that this organization has had for so long."

It came as no surprise that Jones chose Garrett to replace Phillips. After all, he'd been hired as the club's offensive coordinator before Jones even picked Phillips over Norv Turner as the Cowboys' fifth head coach since 1997. Before joining the Cowboys' staff, Garrett spent the last two seasons coaching Miami's quarterbacks. He played in Dallas from 1993 to 1999, appearing in 23 games, starting nine. "The nature and timing of this hire is unique in that we were dealing with a limited window of time in which to talk to Jason about returning to Dallas," Jones said in a statement.

In the three years as the Cowboys' offensive coordinator, Garrett had interviewed for head coaching jobs with Baltimore, Atlanta, and St. Louis, but remained with the Cowboys. After guiding the Cowboys to five wins in their last eight games, Jones hired Garrett, who had a year left on a contract that paid him $3.5 million a year. He received four-year deal worth about $5 million a year.

"It's a hard room to get into, and it's a hard room to stay in," Garrett said at his introductory news conference. "My approach as a player was to be as good as I could be each and every day."

Garrett then went about the business of turning the Cowboys into a club that resembled the team he played for that earned the title, Team of the '90s.

Since buying the Cowboys in 1989, Jones had never selected an offensive lineman in the first round. Garrett changed all that. The Cowboys took left tackle Tyron Smith with the ninth pick of the first round. They took center Travis Frederick with the 31st pick in the 2013 draft after trading down, and they added Zack Martin instead of Jones' preferred player—Texas A&M quarterback Johnny Manziel—with the 16th pick of the first round. Now he had the building blocks to implement the same type of scheme Dallas used in the '90s, when they had the best offensive line in football.

After three consecutive 8–8 seasons, Jones made Garrett fire himself as play-caller. Garrett picked Bill Callahan to replace him, but removed him from the process later in the 2013 season. Garrett hired Scott Linehan, his friend and the man who recommended him to be the quarterbacks' coach with the Miami Dolphins in 2005. He charged Linehan with putting together a run-first offense that took pressure off Tony Romo to make every play. Linehan gave DeMarco Murray the ball a franchise-record 392 times, and he responded with a franchise-record 1,845 yards as the team went 12–4 and won the NFC East title.

Murray signed as a free agent after the season, and it took the Cowboys a year to replace him. They took Ezekiel Elliott in the first round with the fourth pick of the 2016 draft because Garrett viewed him as the player who could make their offense virtually unstoppable. ★

Garrett talks with his quarterback, Tony Romo, before the Cowboys' first preseason game of 2016 against the L.A. Rams on August 13 in Los Angeles.

Why Zeke Made Sense

They Wanted a Runner Like Emmitt

This sounds blasphemous, but it's true. For the Dallas Cowboys to win, they needed to reduce Tony Romo's role in the offense. The more Jason Garrett and the Cowboys' offense asked Tony Romo to do over the years, the less success the Cowboys had because of his propensity to make mistakes. The pressure, real or imagined, to make every play created too many situations in which Romo tried to force plays that didn't exist.

The Cowboys were 37–11 when Romo threw fewer than 30 passes in a game, but 41–38 when he threw more than 30. And that's why Garrett completely changed the Cowboys' philosophical approach heading into the 2014 season. From 2007 to 2013, the Cowboys never ran the ball more than 43 percent of the time.

"I think the best thing that we've done as an organization is we've very purposefully tried to take the burden off our quarterback," Cowboys coach Jason Garrett said five weeks into the 2014 season. "At different times in Tony's career, he's had a lot of burden on him—we haven't played great defense, we haven't been great on the offensive line, we haven't run the ball very well. All of a sudden, the way we're going to move the ball and the way we're going to score points is by throwing it. The best teams in this league, the best teams in any sport, have a burden that is spread around. It's rare that one guy can carry a team."

About a month after the 2013 season ended, Garrett hired Scott Linehan to be his third play-caller in three seasons. Linehan received one directive. "'The No. 1 thing we're going to do is get this running game like the old days,'" Linehan said Garrett told him when they discussed working together. "In his mind, he was talking about the days when he was wearing a uniform. That was loud and clear."

Linehan and the Cowboys use a timing-based passing offense that doesn't use much motion or shifting, so their best players must win one-on-one battles. The offense is based on making sure the best players get the most touches. In 2014 that meant getting the ball to DeMarco Murray and Dez Bryant.

Of the Cowboys' 1,014 plays, Murray or Bryant either ran it, caught it, or were targeted 592 times (58 percent). Murray set single-season franchise records of 392 carries and 1,845 yards rushing, while Bryant caught 88 passes for 1,320 yards and 16 touchdowns.

In 2013 Murray had rushed for 1,121 yards and 5.2 yards per carry, but Garrett still wasn't confident in the Cowboys' running game, which is why the Cowboys often passed in running situations. Drafting Notre

Former Ohio State running back Ezekiel Elliott runs a drill at the NFL scouting combine on February 27, 2016, in Indianapolis.

Dame guard Zack Martin in the first round instead of Jerry Jones' choice, Johnny Manziel, changed all that.

"The players matter," Garrett often says.

The team that hadn't taken an offensive lineman in the first round since Missouri's Howard Richards in 1981, had suddenly drafted three in four years.

Murray left for the Eagles after the 2014 season when Philadelphia offered him almost $20 million more than Dallas. So the Cowboys went with Joseph Randle and Darren McFadden at running back because Garrett, vice president Stephen Jones, and Jerry Jones convinced themselves that anyone could succeed behind their offensive line.

Joseph Randle started the first six games in 2014 but gained more than 65 yards just once, and the Cowboys cut him the week after he asked out of a 27–20 loss to the New York Giants after two carries in 2015. McFadden rushed for 1,089 yards in 10 starts, but he wasn't the kind of dynamic runner that forced teams to alter their defenses. McFadden had five 100-yard games and carried the ball 239 times, but scored only three touchdowns. He wasn't a powerful runner around the goal line, forcing the

Cowboys to settle for too many field goals. In 2014 Murray scored nine of his 13 touchdowns on runs of one, two, or three yards.

The only good thing about the Cowboys 4–12 season in 2015 was that it provided an opportunity to add the kind of dynamic player they never would've had the chance to add if Romo had stayed healthy and the season had gone as planned. The Cowboys, drafting fourth, hadn't planned on having a top 10 draft pick for a while, so they couldn't mess it up. Quarterbacks Jared Goff of California and Carson Wentz of North Dakota State were going 1–2 in the draft no matter who picked them.

Ohio State defensive end Joey Bosa, Florida State cornerback Jalen Ramsey, and Ohio State running back Ezekiel Elliott were the next three best players in the draft. The Cowboys needed a defensive end and cornerback, so whoever San Diego didn't select with the third pick would still leave the Cowboys with a dynamic defensive player: Bosa or Ramsey.

Elliott, though, intrigued the Cowboys after consecutive 1,800-yard seasons at Ohio State. He ran with speed and power, caught the ball naturally, and

Before selecting running back Ezekiel Elliott (opposite page) with the No. 4 pick in the draft, the Cowboys considered taking either Ohio State defensive end Joey Bosa (above left) or Florida State cornerback Jalen Ramsey (above right).

"He's the biggest impact player in the draft. If we're drafting this high, that's who we should take." —Jerry Jones

took a certain joy in blocking, making him nearly as good without the ball as he was with it.

But in today's NFL, the running-back-by-committee approach has marginalized running backs. Only six runners have had more than 300 carries in the past four years, a total Emmitt Smith surpassed seven times when the Cowboys ruled the 1990s.

Garrett knew a ball-control attack with Elliott at the epicenter would work. It's a familiar formula—Bill Parcells used the same formula in 2003, his first season with the Cowboys. Dallas finished second in time of possession (32:53) as quarterback Quincy Carter and running back Troy Hambrick led them to a 10–6 record and a playoff berth after three straight 5–11 seasons. And it's the formula the Cowboys used in 2014, when they finished first in time of possession (32:51) and fifth in points scored (29.2).

Georgia's Todd Gurley and Wisconsin's Melvin Gordon were the only two running backs drafted in the first round from 2013 to 2015. Still, Elliott remained at the top of the Cowboys' draft board. Florida State's Jalen Ramsey was second. Three days before the draft, Garrett spent seven hours looking at every one of Elliott's snaps in 2015 and Ramsey's snaps in 2015, according to *Sports Illustrated*'s Peter King.

Elliott gave the Cowboys an opportunity to recreate the success they had in 2014 with Murray, and Jones has always been a sucker for stars because they make marketing the team easy. "He's the biggest impact player in the draft," Jones said after the draft. "If we're drafting this high, that's who we should take."

Elliott, as you would expect, was thrilled about running behind the league's best offensive line. "After what I've seen on film, they pop those holes open," he said in a conference call, "and the running back gets to that second level so fast and just do what running backs do best. So I'm excited."

So were Garrett and Jones. They saw what Emmitt Smith did for the Cowboys in the 1990s, and now they had another version. ★

Elliott catches a pass during the Cowboys' rookie camp in Irving, Texas, on May 6, 2016.

The Final Choice

Dak Was Not First Choice to Be QB of the Future

Brandon Weeden finally made owner Jerry Jones see the proverbial light. Or, maybe, it was Matt Cassel. They were both awful in 2015, combining to go 1–9 as starters with seven touchdowns and nine interceptions. Their ineffectiveness and Tony Romo's missing all or parts of 14 games with collarbone injuries made Jones and his triumvirate of power brokers—Stephen Jones, Jason Garrett, and Will McClay—decide it was time to draft the quarterback of the future.

The question the Cowboys had to answer revolved around when to take a quarterback, because California's Jared Goff and North Dakota State's Carson Wentz were expected to be taken 1–2 in the draft. The Cowboys would draft fourth, and there wasn't another quarterback worthy of being taken at that spot ahead of Ohio State defensive end Joey Bosa, Ohio State running back Ezekiel Elliott, or Florida State cornerback Jalen Ramsey.

Romo's injury is the only reason the Cowboys were able to draft so high, having gone 4–12 in 2015, a year after they had gone 12–4. This was an opportunity to make the best out of a bad situation, much as the NBA's San Antonio Spurs had done in 1997, when back and foot injuries limited center David Robinson to six games and transformed the Spurs from a championship-caliber team to a lottery team. The Spurs went 20–62 and wound up with the first pick in the draft, which they used to select Tim Duncan. He teamed with Robinson for six seasons before becoming the bridge that helped San Antonio continue its basketball dynasty for another decade.

So, if there had been a quarterback worthy, the Cowboys would've drafted one to secure their future after Romo. Jones had been loath to select quarterbacks during much of his tenure as owner because choosing the wrong player could wreck a franchise for years due to the combination of their high bust rate and huge salaries.

Since drafting Troy Aikman with the No. 1 pick overall in 1989, Jones had not taken another quarterback in the first round. In fact, he had drafted only four at all: Steve Walsh (1989 supplemental draft), Bill Musgrave (1991), Quincy Carter (2001), and Stephen McGee (2009). McGee was the last quarterback the Cowboys took in the draft. The 101st player selected in the 2009 draft lasted three years and 82 passes.

While the Cowboys were scouting players for the draft, they became intrigued with 6'7", 245-pound Memphis quarterback Paxton Lynch. He passed for

Dak Prescott drops back to pass for Mississippi State as a junior versus Auburn on October 11, 2014. Prescott led his No. 3 Bulldogs over the No. 2 Tigers 38–23.

6,807 yards with 50 touchdowns and 13 interceptions his last two seasons. They also studied Penn State's Christian Hackenberg, Michigan State's Connor Cook, Mississippi State's Dak Prescott, and North Carolina State's Jacoby Brissett.

They liked Lynch the most, even though he was going to need time to develop in the NFL, as he played in one of those gimmicky college offenses that didn't require him to make the same types of reads and throws he was going to have to do to succeed at the NFL level. He was clearly a first-round talent, and if the Cowboys could figure out a way to draft Lynch, it would be a perfect match. He could sit on the bench for two or three years, learning from Romo and picking up the nuances of the Cowboys offense. Whenever Romo retired, they could slide him into the starting lineup, making for an easy transition.

It was a perfect plan. They just had to figure out how to acquire Lynch on draft day.

The Cowboys discussed dropping back two spots to No. 6 with the Baltimore Ravens in hopes of adding picks that they could later use to move back into the first round. Garrett was adamant that the Cowboys grab Elliott because he saw a player who could be an even bigger game-changer than DeMarco Murray, who had rushed for 1,845 yards in 2014 before leaving via free agency. The Cowboys didn't want to lose him, and they believed they had to come away with Elliott, Bosa, or Ramsey. Moving to Baltimore's spot created too much risk.

Once the Cowboys took Elliott with the fourth pick in the draft, Lynch became the focus. The Cowboys had privately worked him out in Orlando, Florida, and they'd hosted him during a pre-draft visit at their Valley Ranch training complex. The Cowboys had also hosted quarterbacks Cook, Brissett, Hackenberg, and Prescott at Valley Ranch for pre-draft visits.

After taking Ezekiel Elliott with the No. 4 overall pick in the 2016 draft, the Cowboys set their sights on Memphis quarterback Paxton Lynch (top left). If they couldn't land him, they still liked Penn State's Christian Hackenberg (top center) or Michigan State's Connor Cook (top right). Prescott (opposite) was the Cowboys' fourth choice, and they ended up with him at No. 135.

The Cowboys tried to work out a deal but couldn't make it happen. The owner didn't want to part with the second- and third-round picks Seattle wanted in exchange for giving up the 26ᵗʰ pick in the draft. Dallas offered a second-round pick (No. 34 overall) and a fourth-round pick (No. 101). But the Broncos gave the Seahawks No. 31 overall and No. 94 overall for Seattle's first-round pick and ended up taking Lynch.

"We felt really good about this particular player, and it didn't work out," Stephen Jones said after the draft's first day ended.

Jerry Jones second-guessed himself. "I'm not gonna go jump from Dallas' tallest building, so let's put this in perspective," Jones said the next day. "And I live with second-guessing and disappointments. That's a part of this business. But if I had to do it all over again? I'd give the three. When I look back on my life, I've overpaid for my big successes every time. And when I've tried to get a bargain or get a little cheaper or get a better deal on it, I ended up usually either getting it and not happy I got it, or missing [it]. I probably should have overpaid here."

Prescott, the Cowboys' fourth-round draft pick, works out during the team's rookie camp in Irving, Texas, on May 6, 2016.

"When I look back on my life, I've overpaid for my big successes every time. And when I've tried to get a bargain or get a little cheaper or get a better deal on it, I ended up usually either getting it and not happy I got it, or missing [it]." —Jerry Jones

The Cowboys, determined to get a quarterback, started focusing on Cook at the top of the fourth round. But Oakland, searching for a quality backup behind Derek Carr, moved up one spot ahead of the Cowboys by swapping fourth-round picks and sending a fifth-round pick to the Cleveland Browns. Hackenberg had been taken by the New York Jets in the second round, and Brissett had gone to the New England Patriots in the third round.

Only Prescott remained among the quarterbacks the Cowboys had studied intently. The Cowboys met with Prescott at least four times in three months, including a March 21 trip to Starkville, Mississippi, where quarterbacks coach Wade Wilson gave Prescott a private workout. They also met him at the Senior Bowl (where he was named MVP), the scouting combine, and the Valley Ranch visit.

Even so, the Cowboys took defensive end Charles Tapper with the 101st pick. They didn't take Prescott until the 135th pick. "This is something I dreamed about, running around the house acting like I was a Cowboys quarterback my whole life," Prescott said during a conference call with reporters at Valley Ranch. "For it all to come true, it's such a blessing. Just being here with my family when Mr. Jones gave me that call and just the excitement throughout my family, which the majority of them are Cowboys fans, it was awesome."

As the preseason wound down, the Cowboys no longer lamented missing out on Lynch or Cook. Prescott had earned their trust with a strong off-season and preseason. Prescott is not a player who dazzles in practice. To really understand what makes him an effective leader and player requires constant exposure. His work-ethic, confidence, and demeanor draws others to him.

"I think he has rare leadership and people skills," Jones said. "We had obviously heard he was good. but you never know what that means talking to people. I mean, you do the best you can, talking to coaches and people who have been around him, but we have gotten that on a lot of people. 'He's impeccable. He is this. He is that.' Then it turns around he is not quite impeccable—good but not impeccable—but this guy has been special in terms of that. And then he's got an insatiable appetite to want to learn the game. He doesn't take one rep for granted. He's relentless like that." ★

Zeke's Off-the-Field Drama

The one aspect of the NFL Ezekiel Elliott has not been able to hurdle, run through, or run over is controversy. It has followed Elliott since he arrived in the NFL, whether he's been the victim of circumstance or exercised poor judgment. Those issues, however, have put him in harm's way because the NFL can be unforgiving when it comes to players who bring negative attention to the league.

Commissioner Roger Goodell serves as judge and jury in many cases. He also hears appeals. Find yourself in his office, and trouble can follow because a player doesn't have to commit a crime to face a suspension.

"The scrutiny is there for sure. That's probably the biggest thing," Elliott said, surrounded by media at his locker in September. "The biggest part is mentally blocking it out—not necessarily blocking it out, but focusing on what's important. The outside noise is not really important to us. What's important is what's going on in here because we're the ones out there going to war with each other and we're the ones who have to play with each other. Everything else is trying to get clicks and make stories."

Elliott's job is to not make it so easy.

Three months after the Cowboys drafted Elliott, he was accused of domestic violence by Tiffany Thompson, a former girlfriend. She said Elliott abused her five different times over several days in July 2016. She posted photos of the alleged abuse on Instagram.

The police did not arrest Elliott for the alleged incident, and the city attorney's office later declined to bring charges because of conflicting and inconsistent evidence. The same woman also accused Elliott of domestic violence in Florida five months earlier, telling police there that he had pushed her against a wall. Those allegations did not result in charges either.

The NFL says its investigation remains open. After the Ray Rice scandal in 2014, the NFL is not taking any chances that it has not thoroughly investigated an incident. The NFL gave Rice a two-game suspension. A videotape surfaced showing he had punched his wife, and a public outcry ensued.

When the Cowboys began OTAs in May, the NFL had still not cleared Elliott. "The best way to be fair to a player is to be thorough and to take our time to get it right," Goodell said at the owners meetings in January held at the Las Colinas Four Seasons and Resort. "That is what we're working at. We have professionals who are working on this. We're not putting a timetable on it. We want to make sure that they get it right and get all the facts. When they reach a conclusion, we'll all know about it."

In August, Elliott visited a marijuana shop before a preseason game in Seattle. It's legal to smoke marijuana in Washington state, but it was a bad look, and coach Jason Garrett chastised him. Far too frequently, he's found himself in the news for something other than scoring touchdowns.

Ezekiel Elliott watches organized team activities at the Cowboys' training facility on May 25, 2017, in Frisco, Texas. In March he was caught on video pulling down a woman's shirt at a Saint Patrick's Day party in Dallas.

The NFL says its investigation remains open. After the Ray Rice scandal in 2014, the NFL is not taking any chances.

"You definitely have to think of the perception of things before you actually do certain things," Elliott said of the incident. "It may not seem like it's a big deal to you yourself, but there's a bigger picture. It's definitely a learning experience about the scrutiny. You just have to be careful and not give anybody a chance to say anything."

In January he was involved in a minor car accident four days before the club's playoff game at its training facility and bristled at questions. "I'm fine. I'm healthy. I'm good," Elliott told reporters when he arrived at the facility. "My car is messed up, that's about it. I'm just glad nobody got hurt."

Once the NFL closes its probe, Elliott will stop feeling like the league is out to get him. "I do want closure. I do," Elliott told reporters after the Cowboys' playoff loss to the Green Bay Packers. "I would rather them not drag on as long. I think if there was something to find, which there's not, they would've found it by now. The police did a very thorough investigation. I will

tell you this—it just seems like they're dragging their feet right now. Who knows, man? I just want it to end."

None of this stopped Elliott from leading the NFL in yards or carries, but after his first season it seems only Elliott can stop Elliott.

In February, Elliott was at a bar in Columbus, Ohio, when one of his friends was arrested for trying to take a gun into the establishment. That's not Elliott's fault, but it brought more negative attention.

Then came one of the worst decisions he made since entering the NFL. In a video posted by TMZ Sports in March 2017, Elliott is shown at a St. Patrick's Day party in Dallas pulling down part of a woman's shirt, exposing one of her breasts. In a second video, also posted by TMZ Sports and recorded while Elliott and the woman watched the parade from a rooftop bar, she moves his hand away before pulling her own shirt down. "There is not much that I want to say other than that was unfortunate and not good," owner Jerry Jones told reporters at the owners' meetings. "But it wouldn't

"It's definitely a learning experience about the scrutiny. You just have to be careful and not give anybody a chance to say anything." —Ezekiel Elliott

be the right emphasis one way or the other to get into any communications or dialogue since that happened." Elliott did not face criminal charges, but it was one more indication of poor judgment that could ultimately lead to the NFL choosing to suspend him.

He also missed the first OTA of 2017 after being the passenger in a car that was rear-ended leaving a charity event. Elliott's job is to make better decisions off the field, so he can stay on it.

The trials and tribulations of Elliott's first year in the NFL did teach him one thing about himself. "I think what I learned about myself was my ability to kind of block out outside noise and still be able to go out there and compete, go out there and excel in this game," he said. "I've been through a lot of shit this off-season, still going through a lot of stuff." ★

A Lifetime Goal

Zeke Wants Dickerson's Rushing Record

The pursuit of greatness has never bothered Ezekiel Elliott. It's among the reasons he attended Ohio State University instead of Missouri, where his mom ran track and his dad played football. At Ohio State, a school with seven Heisman Trophy winners, Elliott could never get complacent because he was competing not only against himself but the memories of Archie Griffin and Eddie George.

Elliott loves every aspect of football, from the training to the physicality. He's self-motivated, the kind of player who practices as hard as he plays every day. So, when the Cowboys drafted him with the fourth pick of the first round, the conversations about Eric Dickerson's 33-year-old, single-season rookie rushing record began. The Los Angeles Rams took Dickerson, a 6′3″, 220-pound runner with a dancer's grace and sprinter's speed, with the second pick after the Denver Broncos selected John Elway.

Dickerson dominated the NFL the same way he did college football, surpassing the 100-yard mark nine times, finishing his rookie season with 1,808 yards on 390 carries and 18 touchdowns. "Before the season, me and my roommate had talked about 1,200 or 1,300 yards, but after I did it, I was like, you should have 1,700 or 1,800 yards in a good year," Dickerson said. "That became my standard. Anything less than that and I wasn't playing well."

Dickerson started slowly, gaining 91 yards on 31 carries against the New York Giants, and he failed to gain more than 100 yards in the next two games before coach John Robinson shifted from a split-back to one-back offense. When Dickerson surpassed George Rogers' 1981 rookie rushing record of 1,674 yards, it marked the sixth time in 12 years the record had been broken.

Green Bay's John Brockington set the record in 1971, a year after the NFL-AFL merger with 1,105 yards. San Diego's Don Woods broke it three years later with 1,162 yards. He never gained more than 514 yards during the rest of his eight-year career. Earl Campbell established a new record with 1,450 yards in 1978, O.J. Anderson surpassed it with 1,605 yards in 1979, and George Rogers gained 1,674 yards in 1981.

Then came Dickerson.

Elliott and Dickerson also share an agent, Rocky Arceneaux, which is why the conversation started quickly after the Cowboys selected him. Elliott, the draft's most dynamic running back, was also going to a team with the NFL's best offensive line, and he was going to play for a coach committed to running the ball.

"When I look at that offensive line—man, if I had that offensive line, I'd run for 2,600 yards," a chuckling Dickerson told ESPN. "I might not even need a quarterback. The holes are so gaping big, almost like when Emmitt [Smith] played. You look at them holes,

Ezekiel Elliott runs through an attempted tackle by Browns linebacker Joe Schobert on November 6, 2016, in Cleveland. Elliott ran for 92 yards on 18 carries with two touchdowns in the Cowboys' 35–10 win.

In Week 16 against the Detroit Lions, Elliott rushed for 80 yards and two TDs on 12 carries in the first half. He sat out the second half of the 42–21 Dallas win and didn't play in Week 17 against the Philadelphia Eagles, ending his season with an NFL-leading 1,631 yards.

like, wow. That's a running back's dream. You want an offensive line that has that cohesiveness, that's played together, that knows each other's next move, and that's what they have in Dallas."

With the season rapidly approaching, running backs coach Gary Brown decided to address the issue of the rushing record. On the second floor of the Cowboys new state-of-the-art training facility that opened in August, Brown and Elliott stayed in the running backs meeting room after the others had left a few days before the regular-season opener against the New York Giants. Their conversation lasted a couple of minutes, if that.

"'There's a lot of talk about [the record],'" Brown recalled telling Elliott in an interview with ESPN. "'Let's me and you address it in the room right now and get rid of it. If it happens, it happens. If it doesn't, it doesn't.'"

Elliott said the topic hardly dominated his thoughts. He was more interested in winning games than records. "Coach," said Elliott, "I don't even think that much about it."

Four days before his first game, Elliott stood in the middle of the Cowboys' plush locker room and joked about breaking Dickerson's record. "I know a little bit about him," Elliott said. "Eighteen hundred yards. We joke about it all the time. I told him I'm going to get it. Honestly, yeah, that's something I do want to accomplish, but it's not a priority. What's a priority is going out there and winning ballgames every week."

Dickerson told Elliott to go for it.

"He told me through his agent that he was going to break my record," Dickerson told ESPN. "I just laughed and said, 'Good luck.' Many have said that; all have failed. I like the record because you get one shot at it and that's it, because you're a rookie one time. You don't get three or four shots at that record. 'Oh, let me do it again.' Nah."

While Dickerson's record was the goal, the Cowboys have had such a legacy of running backs, there were plenty of landmarks for him to pass along the way in his quest for Dickerson's Holy Grail. Tony Dorsett and Emmitt Smith set the standard for runners in this franchise. Each is in the Hall of Fame. Elliott surpassed Emmitt Smith's rookie rushing total of 937 yards in Week 10 with 114 yards and touchdown runs of 14 and 32 in the last two minutes as Dallas rallied to beat the Pittsburgh Steelers 35–30.

The next week, he ran for 97 yards on 25 carries in a 27–17 win over the Baltimore Ravens and established a new Cowboys rookie rushing record as he broke Dorsett's 40-year record of 1,007 yards set in 1977.

Elliott needed 258 yards in the last two games to break Dickerson's record. But Elliott knew he'd probably sit out the last game if the Cowboys secured home-field advantage throughout the playoffs.

"It would be special, just to know I had the best rookie season a running back has had in this league, especially a record that's been however old it is," Elliott told ESPN. "It's really not my decision, one. Two, I'm just there to do what they tell me to do. I think there is a shot to get that rookie rushing record, but it's not worth risking what we have the opportunity to do as a team. And I wouldn't want to risk getting it for something we have the opportunity to go and play for a Super Bowl."

He carried 12 times for 80 yards in a 42–21 win over Detroit in Week 16, sitting out the second half and ending his record chase.

Still he led the NFL in rushing yards (1,631) and carries (322).

"I've just learned through experience, you don't focus on [records]," Elliott said. "You focus on going out there and winning ballgames, and good things happen." ★

Elliott hurdles Baltimore cornerback Tavon Young during the Cowboys' 27–17 victory over the Ravens on November 20, 2016, in Arlington, Texas. Elliott established a new Cowboys rookie rushing record in the Week 11 win.

A Forgettable Debut

Cowboys Lose Opener as Dak and Zeke Struggle

There was no anxiety in Dak Prescott's voice. No hint of fear in his words. And there never has been since the day the Cowboys selected him with the 135th pick of the 2016 NFL Draft. When you've been through what Prescott has been through as a sophomore at Mississippi State—watching his mom, Peggy, die from colon cancer—it puts football in perspective.

It's just a game. Life is hard; football is fun.

"I think, 'believe' and 'expect,'" Prescott told reporters four days before his NFL debut. "Believe you're supposed to be there. Expect you're supposed to be there. Expect for good things to happen. Believe that success is going to come when you prepare. I just try to do all those things the best I can, and I know when I go out there no matter what the situation is, what stadium we're in, who we're playing, or what the down and distance is, if I'm prepared for it, I believe I'm going to have success on it. It should happen."

So it didn't affect Prescott when he found out he was going to be the fourth quarterback in the franchise's 57-year history to start as a rookie. And it certainly didn't have any impact on Prescott that he and running back Ezekiel Elliott would be the first rookie quarterback/running back combination to start for the Dallas Cowboys since Roger Staubach and Calvin Hill did it in 1969 (Staubach only started once that season). Those Cowboys went 11–2–1 and won their division before getting pounded by the Cleveland Browns 38–14 in the divisional playoff.

Heading into the opener against the New York Giants, much of the hoopla surrounding the game was focused on Prescott's ability to handle the hoopla surrounding his debut in front of a national television audience. He handled the preseason opener in Los Angeles Coliseum and a crowd of 89,000 with no problems, completing 10 of 12 passes with two touchdowns against the Los Angeles Rams.

In the third preseason game, when he wasn't even supposed to play, Prescott took over for the injured Tony Romo four plays into the game and played well. "I don't think his approach has changed since we met him," Garrett told reporters. "That's one of the things we were most impressed by him. That was the feedback that we got from everybody who had been around him at Mississippi State, the guys who coached him at the Senior Bowl, our experiences with him leading up to the draft, and after we drafted him. He's a very professional guy in his approach."

Cowboys rookie quarterback Dak Prescott throws an incomplete pass through the arms of New York Giants safety Landon Collins in the second half of Prescott's NFL debut, a 20–19 Dallas loss on September 11, 2016.

While Prescott was the epicenter of the pregame focus, few questions existed about Elliott. He had been spectacular in the third preseason game against Seattle and, like Prescott, didn't play in the final preseason game.

The Giants entered the game as one-point favorites, even though the Cowboys had beaten their NFC East rivals five straight times for the first time since 1992–1994. The Cowboys were 8–0 all-time against the Giants in openers, a streak that began in 1965 and spanned each of the Cowboys' eight coaches and nine presidents from Lyndon Johnson to Barack Obama.

The Giants, coming off consecutive 6–10 seasons, spent the off-season fortifying their defense to take some of the burden off Eli Manning. Conservative GM Jerry Reese changed his fiscal approach and spent plenty of cash to fix their defense with big-money additions such as pass-rusher Olivier Vernon, defensive tackle and run-stopper Damon Harrison, and cornerback Janoris Jenkins.

Prescott, the 134th quarterback since 1980 to debut as a starter, was trying to become one of only 43 to win his debut. Quarterbacks Troy Aikman, Peyton Manning, and Russell Wilson all began their careers 0–1 but eventually won the Super Bowl.

For this organization, that can be the only goal.

Prescott seemed comfortable in the pocket and didn't force throws to Dez Bryant, the Cowboys' best receiver. The Giants' defensive coordinator, Steve Spagnuolo, devised a game plan designed to test Prescott's patience.

While Prescott played well, Elliott looked slow and sluggish. He carried 15 times for 31 yards in the first half. There were few holes, but Alfred Morris, who carried seven times for 35 yards, looked considerably better. "I'm used to running against the New York

Cowboys first-round draft pick Ezekiel Elliott is brought down by Giants safety Darian Thompson (bottom) and defensive end Kerry Wynn (top) in the first half of the Cowboys' loss. Elliott was held to 51 yards on 20 carries and one touchdown in his regular season rookie debut.

Despite a mediocre passer rating of 69.4 in his first game, Prescott still had a chance to come from behind in the fourth quarter of the Cowboys' one-point loss to NFC East rival Giants.

"We're going to stick behind him, rally behind him, and he's going to be a monster, that's what we all believe." —Dez Bryant

Giants. I know their scheme and what they're doing," Morris told reporters. "I was just able to find holes. I was able to get a little more rhythm than Zeke was able to get."

Give some credit to the Giants for limiting Elliott to 51 yards on 20 carries. But Elliott also created his own issues because he did a poor job with his fundamentals. "I think I was average, you know. Average," Elliott said. "That's not why I was brought here, to be average, so we've got a lot of work to get done."

Emmitt Smith gained two yards on two carries in his debut but wound up as the NFL's all-time leading rusher with 18,355 yards. Tony Dorsett had 11 yards on four carries in his first game and wound up in the Hall of Fame with more than 12,000 yards. DeMarco Murray, who owns the franchise's single-season record with 1,845 yards, had two carries for no yards in his debut. Only Herschel Walker (64 yards) and Hill (70 yards) had more productive debuts than Elliott with the Cowboys.

Still, there was one eight-yard run where he showed all the skills that made the Cowboys take him with the fourth pick. From the New York 8, Elliott started left and cut back right, eluding the middle linebacker, then accelerated through a hole and dove into the end zone.

While New York forced Prescott to make conservative throws with their coverages, and their defense controlled Elliott, the Giants took a 20–19 lead with 6:13 left. Prescott had an opportunity to make this the most memorable debut ever for a Cowboys rookie starter when he took over at the Dallas 25 with no timeouts. "That's what I wanted," Prescott said. "I'm thinking, go win the game. I'd rather have it in my hands than in Eli's hands with that time on the clock."

After going nowhere, Dallas got the ball back with 1:05 on the clock. Mistakes ruined the drive. Tight end Jason Witten dropped a pass, Zack Martin was penalized for a false start, Terrance Williams tried to gain additional yards instead of getting out of bounds, and time expired before the Cowboys could attempt a field goal.

Prescott completed 25 of 45 passes for 227 yards and a 69.4 passer rating.

"He's a hell of a football player. The ultimate competitor. We love him," Dez Bryant said after the game. "We're going to stick behind him, rally behind him, and he's going to be a monster, that's what we all believe." ★

A Month for the Ages

Four Games That Made Zeke a Star

For two weeks, Ezekiel Elliott had heard them all—the haters, the doubters, the emotionally invested fans on social media who questioned his ability—and there wasn't a whole lot he could say about it.

He averaged less than three yards a carry in his debut, a loss to the New York Giants, and had been benched for the last six minutes of his second game, a win over the Washington Redskins, after fumbling for a second time. A segment of fans and media were already calling for Alfred Morris, an off-season free-agent acquisition, to log more playing time, and questions were being bandied about over whether Elliott was going to be a bust like former Alabama star Trent Richardson, the third player taken in the 2012 draft.

Elliott touched the ball 653 times—rushing, receiving, and returns—in his three-year career at Ohio State and fumbled just four times. The reality is Elliott's fumbles against Washington distracted from the substance of his performance. He finished the 27–23 win over Washington with 83 yards on 21 carries and his first two 20-yard runs of the season.

Seven days later, on *Sunday Night Football*, that changed. That's the night he became an NFL star.

Elliott came to the league equipped with all of the intangibles necessary to become a star. He has an effervescent personality that draws fans and teammates to him whether we're talking about a 14-year veteran like Jason Witten or a fellow rookie like Dak Prescott. He smiles broadly and often. And when he signs memorabilia for fans, he greets them warmly and looks them in the eye whether he's talking to a wide-eyed youngster missing a front tooth at Point Mugu Naval Air Base less than an hour after the Cowboys arrive in California for training camp or if he's posing for a photo with a fan after his second practice of the day.

But it was on that Sunday night against the Chicago Bears, with 14:21 left in the fourth quarter, that he showed what he could do on the field in an NFL game. On first-and-10 from the Dallas 29, Elliott sped around right end, changing his stride subtly as Bears safety Chris Prosinski approached him. As Prosinski lowered his shoulders to tackle Elliott, the former Missouri state champion in the 110-meter and 300-meter hurdles leapt over his defender using perfect technique and wound up with a 14-yard gain. "Whenever you get a DB in the open field with open space, he's going to cut tackle," Elliott said after the game. "So I thought I might have to pull the hurdle out. Sometimes, you run over a

Ezekiel Elliott hurdles Chicago Bears safety Chris Prosinski on his way to a 14-yard gain in the fourth quarter of the Cowboys' 31–17 win on *Sunday Night Football*. Elliott finished the game with 140 yards on 30 carries.

guy. Sometimes, you give him a move. Sometimes, you hurdle him. You gotta keep changing it up, so the defense doesn't know what you're going to do."

The move stunned Dez Bryant. "I was standing right next to him, and when he did it, I was like, *Zeke just jumped over this mother——!*" Bryant said laughing near his locker in the Cowboys' locker room.

Minutes later, the gifs and photoshopped images of Elliott hurdling everything from the Grand Canyon to the Statue of Liberty to a T-rex in *Jurassic Park* began showing up all over social media. Even Elliott's mom, Dawn, posted a picture on Twitter of her hurdling in college side-by-side with a photo of Elliott hurdling in high school. The former heptathlete taught her only son how to hurdle.

The run came near the end of a 30-carry, 140-yard performance in a 31–17 win over the Bears before a national TV audience. He started the game with a 21-yard run up the middle, and the Bears never slowed him down. For those wondering if his game against Chicago was a fluke or the product of playing against a bad defense, Elliott's performance over the next three weeks answered each and every question about his ability.

During a four-game stretch that started against Chicago and ended with a win in Green Bay, Elliott carried 96 times for 569 yards and three touchdowns, while averaging 5.93 yards per carry. The second week, Elliott ripped off 138 yards on 23 carries against San Francisco followed by 134 yards on 15 carries, including a 60-yard touchdown run, against the Cincinnati Bengals. Then came 28 carries for 157 yards against the Green Bay Packers, as he became the first rookie in NFL history to have four consecutive games of more than 130 yards.

In a franchise that has two Hall of Fame runners—Emmitt Smith and Tony Dorsett—and another back in

Elliott breaks loose for a 60-yard touchdown run against the Cincinnati Bengals on October 9, 2016.

Elliott runs for a first down in the second half of the Cowboys' 30–16 win over the Packers on October 16, 2016, in Green Bay. The Cowboys running back rumbled for 157 yards on 28 carries, his fourth straight game gaining 130 or more yards, an NFL rookie record.

Elliott's most impressive performance came against the Green bay Packers, a unit that led the NFL in rushing defense.

Herschel Walker who ranked second in NFL history in all-purpose yards when he retired after the 1998 season, no Cowboys runner had ever had a more productive four-game streak.

In 1993, the year he rushed for 1,486 yards, Smith gained 550 yards on 106 carries during a four-game stretch from October 10 to November 7. The only time Dorsett had four consecutive 100-yard games occurred in 1979, when he gained 478 yards on 85 carries with four touchdowns, while averaging 5.62 from September 30 to October 21.

Elliott's most impressive performance came against the Green bay Packers, a unit that led the NFL in rushing defense. In the first four games of the season, the Packers had allowed an average of 42.8 yards per game and 2.0 yards per carry. Elliott had 12 carries for 60 yards in the first half as the Cowboys built a 17–6 lead. In the fourth quarter, as the Cowboys were trying to clinch the victory, Elliott made his favorite run of the season. On first-and-10 from the Green Bay 26, the Cowboys lined up with one running back and tight ends Gavin Escobar in the left slot, Jason Witten lined up as a wingback on the left, and Geoff Swaim next to right tackle Doug Free. Receiver Lucky Whitehead went in motion from left to right, and when the ball was snapped, Witten ran across the formation but missed his block on right defensive end Julius Peppers.

No worries.

Elliott stiff-armed Peppers at the Green Bay 28 and zoomed around right end. He hurdled LaDarius Gunter at the Packers' 22 but maintained his balance and ran through arm tackles from linebackers Blake Martinez and Jake Ryan and safety Morgan Burnett along the right sideline. Then Elliott dragged Burnett and Martinez another eight yards before getting shoved out of bounds. "It was my favorite run," Elliott told ESPN.com.

Why?

"It showed a little bit of everything I can do," he said with a smile. "It had a stiff-arm, and I showed some speed. Then I hurdled a guy and ran through a couple others before they got me down."

Not only did Elliott's big day lead to a 30–16 win over the Packers, it fueled the first conversations about Elliott being capable of gaining more than 2,000 yards and breaking Eric Dickerson's rookie rushing record of 1,808 yards.

Six games into the season, Elliott led the NFL with 703 yards rushing. The haters, critics, and keyboard cowards on social media had been silenced. ★

Dak's Faith-Based Journey to QB

The word MOM is tattooed on the inside of Dak Prescott's left wrist in block letters. The "O" contains a shaded ribbon, forever a reminder that she died of cancer. He covers the tattoo each Sunday with white trainer's tape and writes the word "faith" on the tape, a tangible reminder of Peggy Prescott's greatest gift to him.

Prescott died of colon cancer in November 2013. Before she died, she equipped her three sons with the intangible qualities they'd need to succeed without her to guide them. She already showed them the importance of work ethic and sacrifice, working long hours at a truck stop to support them and returning to her home at Pine Creek Mobile Estates to cook dinner. In the process, she rarely missed football practices or games. They were important to her because they were important to them, so she found a way.

She became sick during Prescott's sophomore year in college and gave him a message that continues to resonate with him in every meeting, practice, and game with the Cowboys just like it did at Mississippi State. "Let me be your story," she told him. "All the great ones have one."

Prescott told the *Dallas Morning News* that he knew his mom was ill before she delivered the life-changing news. "It was just the woman she was," Prescott said.

"I think she was scared of how it was going to affect me. Obviously, I wanted to go home and be with her, but her words were, 'No, you're not coming back here. You're right where you want to be, and that's where I want you to be.' That obviously allowed me to go out there and clear my mind and just play ball."

In the months before she died, she met with Bishop Anthony Grant, a family friend, to plan her service and ask him to guide her boys as they journeyed through life without her. Grant used 2 Timothy 4:6–7 as the foundation for Peggy's eulogy. It reads, "…the time for my departure is near. I have fought the good fight, I have finished the race, I have kept the faith."

During the service, Grant told the *Morning News* that Peggy assigned one of the scripture's key words to each of her sons. Peggy gave Tad "Fight" because he always fights for the family, and she gave Jace "Finish" because that's what he does once he commits to something.

To Dak, she assigned "Faith" because his belief in achieving his dreams had always been unbreakable. Prescott has FIGHT tattooed along the back of his left shoulder blade and FINISH along the back of his right shoulder blade. "With every struggle, within my life or on the field, I get back up because it's a step closer to what she wanted me to be," he said. "The pain I've

Dak Prescott points to the sky after scoring on a seven-yard run in the Cowboys' 29–23 overtime win against the Philadelphia Eagles on October 30, 2016.

"I wanted to play for the Dallas Cowboys…this moment, right here, is what she dreamt for me."

—Dak Prescott

endured crawled in my heart and molded me into a competitor who won't back down from any fight. From all the times she sat in the stands to all the times I say I wanted to play for the Dallas Cowboys…this moment, right here, is what she dreamt for me."

But it hasn't come without the work ethic she instilled in him from the time he was a child trying to keep up with his older brothers. Prescott has never been that athlete destined for stardom. He's never been the guy so talented he could take shortcuts. He's always had to grind and prepare for opportunity because he's never been the guy sitting on the top of the depth chart when he arrived, whether it was Haughton High School, Mississippi State, or the Dallas Cowboys. We're talking about a three-star high school athlete and a fourth-round pick in the NFL Draft excelling.

But faith has always played an important role in his life. He's always believed God had a plan for his athletic career—even if it wasn't always clear to him. So Prescott has always worked as hard as he could until the plan was revealed.

It's no coincidence that injury has paved the way for him to play in high school, college, and the NFL. And once he entered the starting lineup, he never relinquished the job. In high school, he replaced Matt Smith. At Mississippi State, it was Tyler Russell. Each was a senior at the time they were replaced. Both times, Prescott was a sophomore.

Smith broke a bone on the ring finger of his throwing hand goofing around in practice after a busted play. Russell, a *Parade* All-American from Meridian, Mississippi, ranks fourth on Mississippi State's career passing list with 5,441 yards. His 42 career touchdown passes trails only Prescott's 70.

But in the 2013 season opener, Russell suffered a concussion, paving the way for Prescott to play. When the season ended, Prescott had passed for nearly 2,000 yards with 10 touchdowns and seven interceptions. He passed for 56 touchdowns and 16 interceptions over the next two seasons.

And with the Cowboys, Prescott replaced Tony Romo. His title changed from backup to starter, but Prescott didn't change. His circle of friends remains the same, and he occasionally FaceTimes with them at his locker, reminiscing about the good old days or planning visits.

Prescott insists not much else has changed. "You guys want to talk to me more," Dak said, surrounded by reporters. "Maybe more followers and stuff on Instagram and Twitter. But other than that, my personal life is still the same: same close friends and family that sticks around, and still doing the same things I used to do. I've never really cared or bought into the fame."

That's because his mom raised him on a foundation of faith. ★

Prescott points to heaven after scoring a touchdown in the first half of a game against Kentucky on October 24, 2015. He began pointing skyward in remembrance of his mother after she died during his sophomore year at Mississippi State.

Questions Dak Answered Along the Way

The first answer came in the Dallas Cowboys' first preseason game, a mostly meaningless contest in the Los Angeles Coliseum.

Dak Prescott, a fourth-round pick, who was supposed to spend the season holding a clipboard and learning the nuances of playing in the NFL, suddenly found himself elevated to backup quarterback after Kellen Moore broke his leg the first week of training camp. And he was starting the preseason opener because the Cowboys wanted to protect starter Tony Romo from harm. Prescott did well, completing 10 of 12 passes for 139 yards and two touchdowns, but his performance was about much more than statistics. Prescott's teammates wanted to see how the rookie handled the huddle and the moment.

"The first time he played against the Rams, I knew he was going to be all right no matter what role he had because he wasn't scared," cornerback Orlando Scandrick said. "It was just a preseason game, but you could tell. Nothing bothered him."

That was simply the first of many tests Prescott passed on his journey to prove he could replace Romo and lead the Cowboys in 2016 and beyond. The seemingly flawless way Prescott handled every situation, the more the front office, coaching staff, and players believed in him.

Once the regular season began, the questions seemed to come on a weekly basis.

It began with the New York Giants: how would he handle the opener against a quality opponent? Prescott was solid in a losing effort, completing 25 of 45 passes for 227 yards without a touchdown or an interception. Despite the loss, Prescott looked comfortable throughout the game and gave no indication he couldn't handle the starting job. The next week against Washington, he showed he could lead a fourth-quarter comeback on the road as the Cowboys beat Washington 27–23 to notch their first win. "I wanted to scream, jump up and down, run all around," said Prescott, describing his emotions as the game ended. "I was just excited to get that first win."

Before Prescott left the field, Dez Bryant gave the rookie quarterback a long hug and delivered a message. "Keep leading," he whispered. "Keep balling. Keeping doing what you're doing."

Two weeks later, Prescott rallied the Cowboys again as they overcame a 14–0 second-quarter deficit to beat the 49ers in San Francisco 24–17 and move to 3–1. The Cowboys traveled to Green Bay, where they had only won four times since 1960, on October 16. They had been outscored by an average of 25–16 in those games, so this was expected to be yet another test—even with quarterback Aaron Rodgers struggling.

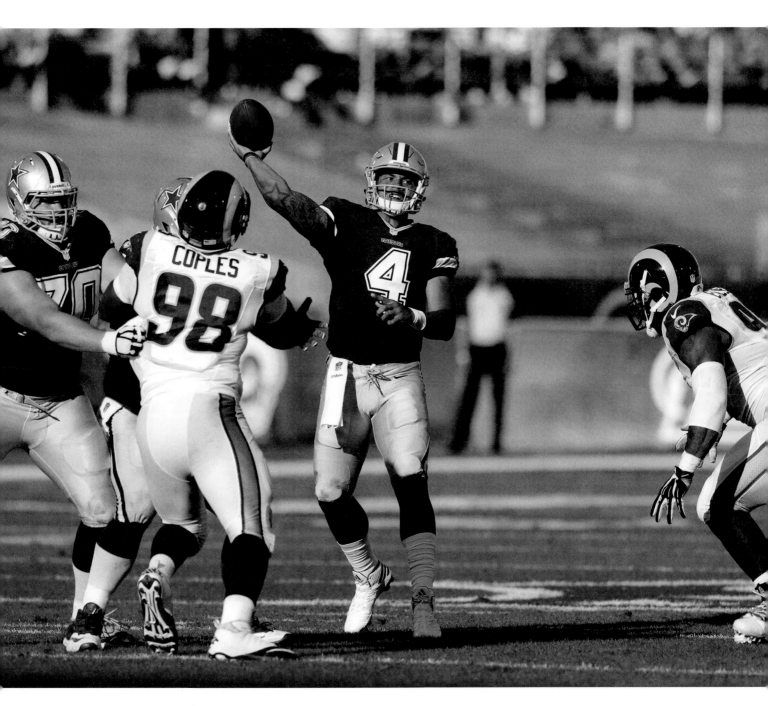

Dak Prescott throws a pass in his NFL debut, the Cowboys' first preseason game of 2016 against the Los Angeles Rams on August 13. Prescott completed 10 of 12 passes for 139 yards and two TDs in the game.

All Prescott did was pass for 247 yards and three touchdowns in a 30–16 win. In the process, he broke New England quarterback Tom Brady's NFL record of 162 passes without an interception at the start of a career. The streak ended at 176 passes when Morgan Burnett intercepted Prescott's third-quarter pass intended for Jason Witten.

"I feel that it is a foundation builder," owner Jerry Jones said.

The best quarterbacks figure out how to win games when they're not playing well. Doing so is a sign of mental toughness, and that's what Prescott displayed in front of a national TV audience on *Sunday Night Football* following a bye week. For three quarters,

Prescott (above) dives into the end zone for a touchdown against the Washington Redskins in the second half of the Week 2 Cowboys victory, the team's first win of 2016 and the first for Prescott as a starting QB in the NFL. Prescott (right) drops back to pass versus the Philadelphia Eagles on October 30, 2016.

Prescott was beyond awful against Philadelphia, completing eight of 19 passes for 152 yards and an interception. The Eagles' pass rush harassed him into mistakes, and the constant pressure resulted in several errant throws as the Eagles took a 23–13 fourth-quarter lead. Instead of folding under the Eagles' relentless pass rush, however, Prescott found a rhythm and completed 11 of his last 20 passes for 135 yards and a couple of touchdowns as the Cowboys rallied to win 29–23 in overtime.

"He plays with the same mentality, the same demeanor, the same temperament regardless of what's happened before," Jason Garrett said after the game. "The best players I've been around were able to do that. He was outstanding at the end of this ballgame."

With each Cowboys win, more questions surfaced about whether Romo would reclaim his starting job once healthy. Prescott handled the situation masterfully, refusing to let the situation divide the locker room or become a distraction. After Prescott led the Cowboys to a 35–30 win in Pittsburgh—the Cowboys rallied twice in the final two minutes—Romo conceded the job two days later on a Tuesday afternoon at the club's $1.5 billion training facility. It's not like Romo had much choice. After all, the Cowboys had won seven straight games, and Prescott had been phenomenal. He had completed 66.7 percent of his passes for 2,339 yards, 14 touchdowns, two interceptions, and a passer rating of 106.2, while averaging 9.0 yards per attempt.

Now the only question left centered on whether Prescott could lead the Cowboys to the NFC East title and homefield throughout the playoffs. The Cowboys were 11–1 and riding a franchise-best 11-game winning streak when they played the New York Giants for the second time. A victory would give the Cowboys the NFC East title, but the Giants shut Prescott down. He completed just 17 of 37 passes for 165 yards in the 10–7 loss as the Cowboys posted season lows in points (seven) and yards (260) and matched their season low in first downs (13).

As expected, Romo's name came up after the game.

"No," Garrett said, when asked if he considered playing Romo. "We feel good about Dak playing quarterback for us."

Jerry Jones also reasserted his confidence in Prescott. "I feel good about our quarterback, and I like where we are at the quarterback position," Jones said after the game. "I don't want to make excuses. Most of what happened to us tonight was a well-coached New York Giants defense."

Now the focus shifted to Romo. All week, Romo supporters wanted to know what it would take for the Cowboys to replace Prescott with the NFL's most polarizing quarterback. Coincidentally, Adidas unveiled a national ad in which Prescott took a shot at his doubters prior to the Tampa Bay game. He turned in one of his best performances of the season, completing a career-high 88.9 percent of his passes (32-of-36) for 279 yards in a 26–20 win before a national TV audience on *Sunday Night Football*.

"I don't pay attention to the noise," Prescott said after the game. "I couldn't tell you what was said all week, but I kind of found out about some stuff later in the week. But it doesn't really bother me. If anything, it's motivation. I just wanted to perform after the game I played last week. I just wanted to respond after my performance."

It was the last question he needed to answer until the playoffs. ★

Prescott scrambles out of the pocket against the Tampa Bay Buccaneers, in one of his best games of the season.
He completed 32 of 36 passes for 279 yards in the 26–20 Cowboys win on *Sunday Night Football*.

How Dak Won Over the Cowboys Locker Room

Even Though Romo Had It for a Decade

Tony Romo led the Cowboys locker room for a decade. Rookie Dak Prescott took it over in less than three months, which might just be his most remarkable achievement in 2016.

Prescott became one of the Cowboys' leaders because he didn't try to impress anybody in the locker room—and that's why he fit in. Some guys try so hard to be leaders, it rubs their teammates the wrong way. You have to earn the right to be a leader; it's not something a coach can anoint a player.

Prescott did it with hard work, learning the offense quickly and practicing at a tempo that often drew praise from coach Jason Garrett and his teammates. He spoke up, the way leaders do, when plays weren't executed properly, whether the criticism was directed at a starter such as Dez Bryant or a practice squad rookie like Andy Jones.

Prescott earned a degree from Mississippi State in educational psychology and a master's degree in workforce leadership. He understands, intellectually and psychologically, the dynamics of the locker room and the delicate nature of team chemistry. "It's kind of who I am," Prescott told a small group of reporters as he sat in his locker discussing the importance of leadership one Thursday in December. "If we're doing a class project, then I'm going to be the one talking and taking the lead. I might not necessarily put all of the work in the project, but I want to help and do as much as I can and get everyone going in the right direction. If somebody says I'm a leader or notices the things I try to do to be a leader, it's the ultimate compliment. To me, for a teammate or peer to call you a leader means a lot because they're going to look up to you and they're going to follow you."

Prescott could've found himself in the epicenter of a quarterback controversy because being quarterback of the Dallas Cowboys is among the highest-profile jobs in sports. But he handled all the questions about whether it was Tony Romo's team with grace and aplomb, while letting his play provide the biggest statements.

He related to the core of players better than Romo, which shouldn't really surprise anyone. Romo was a 36-year-old family man who missed all or part of 12 of

Dak Prescott during practice at the Cowboys' training facility in Frisco, Texas, on October 26, 2016.

16 games in 2015 and spent the first eight games of 2016 recovering from a back injury. The result? More than half the players on the roster had never really played with Romo, so they didn't have any loyalty to him.

Plus, Prescott gets it. He's the guy who invited Ezekiel Elliott on the stage with him after he won Offensive Rookie of the Year, and the first words out of his mouth were, "Do you have a knife so I can cut this in half?"

"'Preciate it, 'preciate it," Elliott said as he put his left arm around his quarterback's neck.

Later, Prescott expounded on why he wanted Elliott on the stage with him. "Obviously, I couldn't have done it without him. The defense was homing in on him, making my job easier," Prescott told reporters. "He deserves it just as much as I do from his yards, his catches, the way we handled things in the backfield, it was always together. Without Zeke, I don't win that."

Prescott didn't have to say that, and no one would've blamed him if he had taken that particular moment for himself. Instead he shared the moment with his friend and running back, who was every bit as

Prescott (left) smiles as he and Ezekiel Elliott (right) do a postgame interview after the Cowboys' victory against the Washington Redskins in Arlington, Texas.

Tony Romo, still recovering from a back injury, watches Prescott run a drill during practice. The star quarterback, who led the Cowboys for 10 years, still hoped to return as the team's starting QB.

deserving. In the process, he made a strong friendship even stronger. This is the same guy who helped Dez Bryant work through the death of his father, sad news he found out as the team charter landed in Pittsburgh the day before a game against the Steelers. Prescott talked to Dez about how he channeled the emotions after his mom's death.

The 23-year-old quarterback was also thoughtful enough to send Troy Aikman a birthday text and flowers to Emmitt Smith after his mother died. "You have to have him in your building to understand just how special that young man is," scouting director Will McClay said on SiriusXM NFL Radio. "I'd be kidding if I said we knew Dak was going to be this good and do what he did, because we would've picked him in the first round."

Prescott keeps a huge bag of candy—miniature Twix, Snickers, Milky Way, and M&Ms—tucked behind

After Prescott won the 2016 AP Offensive Rookie of the Year award in February 2017, he invited Elliott to come up on stage with him and said, "Do you have a knife so I can cut this in half?" Prescott later said, "I couldn't have done it without him."

"[H]e's done everything you would want in your quarterback every step of the way." —Jason Witten

some workout gear in his locker and another hidden in the equipment room. Occasionally, he'll walk around the locker room handing out chocolate to offensive and defensive linemen. Prescott hangs out in the locker room, something Romo rarely did, which gives him unscripted opportunities to bond with his teammates. Prescott works the locker room like a presidential candidate, shaking hands with this player, joking with another, and going over a play from practice with another. Offensive players, defensive players—Prescott makes sure he touches all of them. It's no accident. He eagerly participates in "laundry basketball," a favorite lunchtime pastime, in which players shoot a basketball-sized tennis ball into laundry hampers.

"I can go at each different checkbox you write down," said Jason Witten on a fall Thursday in front of his locker. "How does he handle Mondays? How does he handle adversity? How's he handle success? And you just check it off because he's done everything you would want in your quarterback every step of the way."

This is the part of the job that has nothing to do with statistics or audibles, but it's every bit as important to winning. The relationships Prescott builds during the week help on Sundays. Early in a win over Cleveland, Bryant was about to have a meltdown because officials did not call a pass-interference penalty against cornerback Joe Haden. "I've got to manage the offense and that includes managing the people, the attitudes, and emotions," Prescott said after the game. "Dez is a guy we need. We don't need him getting emotional. They're going to hold him. We know that. Flags are going to come and they might not come, but we can't let that affect our game."

Bryant respected the message. "That's real, true leadership," he said.

"Always want to come in and be optimistic," Prescott said, "always with a smile on my face to show the people that need that energy that they can get it from me. ... I just believe in myself. I believe I get around people, I have fun, I show them the difference of having fun and then being locked in and handling your business. That allows people to gravitate toward you and know we can joke. We can joke, but as soon as it's time for football, we all lock in and get focused on our job. It's just something I try to live my life by every day—having fun, but when it's business, it's strictly business."

"He's shown leadership," said Witten. "It's a great trait. Part of who he is as an individual and his life experiences have allowed him to embrace that." ★

Dak's Worst Game

Joe Montana never had a perfect game. Neither has Tom Brady nor Roger Staubach. Nor Troy Aikman. Perfection at the game's toughest position doesn't exist. It never has, despite what some fans seem to think.

So, while Dak Prescott was leading the Cowboys to 11 consecutive wins and eight straight games with more than 400 yards of total offense—both franchise records—no one expected him to be flawless all season. But he had been nearly perfect heading into yet another big game in a season full of the big games for the rookie with no margin for error.

As Romo recovered from a compression fracture that forced him to be inactive for the first nine games of the season, Prescott completed 67.8 percent of his passes for nearly 3,000 yards with 19 touchdowns and two interceptions through Week 13. He also ran for five touchdowns. Romo, however, had built a loyal following in 10 years as a starter, and the debate raged in barber shops, office buildings, and on sports talk radio shows about whether Romo or the rookie was more qualified to lead the Cowboys to playoff success.

And it didn't help that Jerry Jones kept hinting about Romo being a viable replacement. As much as the front office and coaching staff believed in Prescott, they had seen what Romo could do—and there was still time to make a move back to him, if necessary.

Prescott and the offense had been largely unproductive in a 17–15, come-from-behind win on the road against Minnesota. Prescott had completed 12 of 18 passes for 139 yards and a touchdown. The Romo Apologists grew louder, desperately yearning for Romo to replace Prescott. That was the backdrop as Prescott made his first trip to Giants Stadium.

On a 32-degree night with 95 percent humidity, Prescott easily played his worst game of the season. He had played poorly for three quarters against Philadelphia in October, but played his best ball in the fourth quarter and overtime as the Cowboys rallied to win. But he never found a rhythm against the Giants as defensive coordinator Steve Spagnuolo's unit pressured him all night long. The Giants sacked him three times and hit him nine other times. They never let him get comfortable in the pocket, and his accuracy suffered because he seldom a chance to set his feet. The Cowboys had season lows in yards (260), first downs (13), and points in the 10–7 loss to the Giants. They converted just one of 15 third downs.

Prescott completed just 17 of 37 passes for 165 yards and had the first two-interception game of his career. The man who had posted a passer rating of more than 100 in 10 of 12 games finished with a passer rating of 45.4.

It didn't start off badly for Prescott, whose 31-yard touchdown pass to Terrence Williams on a beautifully designed play resulted in a 7–0 lead on their second possession. On second-and-10 from the New York 31, the Cowboys lined up with two receivers on the left. At

Dak Prescott is pressured by the New York Giants defense as he tries to find an open receiver.

the snap, they faked a toss left to Elliott, and Williams, lined up in the slot, ran right diagonally across the field as all eyes on defense followed Elliott. A wide-open Williams caught the ball in stride at the 5 and breezed into the end zone. That ended the good times.

The defense created a rare turnover—Sean Lee's sack and Cedric Thornton's fumble recovery—at the Dallas 32, but Prescott threw an interception four plays later when Dez Bryant slipped on his route and Janoris Jenkins intercepted the pass. It was his first interception since October 30.

Another sack/fumble recovered by Sean Lee at the Dallas 49 with 7:26 left in the second quarter positioned Dallas to again extend its lead, but the drive fizzled when Prescott was sacked and fumbled on third and 11, ending the drive.

The Giants sacked Prescott three times and never let him get comfortable during the Cowboys' 10–7 loss on December 11, 2016.

Prescott goes down, sacked by the Giants' Robert Thomas (99) and Romeo Okwara (78) in the first half of the game.

"He's got 13 NFL ballgames at a high level under his belt, and what's he got, four interceptions now? Four? I feel good about our quarterback." —Jerry Jones

Still, the Cowboys led 7–0 at halftime. A 39-yard field goal by Robbie Gould pulled the Giants to within four at 7–3 with 5:50 left in the third quarter. On their next possession, Odell Beckham Jr. turned a quick slant into a 61-yard catch-and-run as the Giants took a 10–7 lead with 1:07 left in the third quarter. No big deal. Prescott had rallied the Cowboys to fourth-quarter wins in road games against Washington, Minnesota, and Pittsburgh. Well, the Cowboys had the ball twice in the last 2:39 and didn't come close to scoring.

On third-and-6 from the Dallas 28, Prescott found Bryant on a slant in the middle for a 10-yard gain. It was his first catch of the game, but Jenkins punched the ball loose as Bryant fell to the ground and safety Landon Collins recovered. "It was just an unfortunate situation. I'm at a loss for words," Bryant said after the game. "I can't believe it came out, but it did. We made too many mistakes, and it cost us."

The Cowboys forced a punt that was downed at the Dallas 3. Prescott, under duress on four consecutive downs, did not complete a pass, and the Cowboys turned the ball over on downs. "It's not Dak's bad night," Bryant said. "It's our bad night. We all made mistakes. Don't start that."

The star receiver was doing his best to be supportive. He knew after the loss and Prescott's rough night, the chatter would start early Monday morning about whether Romo needed to regain his starting job after consecutive subpar performances from the offense.

"He's got 13 NFL ballgames at a high level under his belt, and what's he got, four interceptions now? Four? I feel good about our quarterback," owner Jerry Jones told reporters. "And I like where we are at the quarterback position. Most of what happened to us tonight was a well-coached New York Giants defense."

Jason Garrett also diffused any potential quarterback controversy after the game. This is when Garrett's at his best because he's pragmatic to a fault when it comes to his decision-making. He understood Prescott wasn't the primary reason the Cowboys lost, so there was no need to make a change at the position. "The most important thing for us as a football team is you have to be careful looking at the results of games," Garrett said after the loss. "You have to try to get better. There were a lot of good things that we've done over the course of these first 12 weeks of the season. We keep trying to grow and get better."

Prescott understood the situation, and he didn't run from it. The playoffs loomed, and he needed to play better. "You don't have to say much, I'm hard on myself," Prescott said after the game. "I'm my biggest critic." ★

A Game for the Ages

Zeke Gains 209 All-Purpose Yards in Come-from-Behind Win

The play offensive coordinator Scott Linehan called didn't require much imagination. Talk to any coordinator, and he'll tell you that on second-and-18 there are only two choices to make: screen or draw. The idea is to use a safe run or draw that might pick up 10 yards, if you're lucky, and set up a more manageable situation on third down.

So when Linehan sent the play in, he wasn't expecting what happened to happen. Then again, it's rare for a unit to execute the play exactly the way the coach draws it up in the meeting room. But it happened three times against the Pittsburgh Steelers, and each time Ezekiel Elliott scored a touchdown as the Cowboys won their eighth straight game.

Elliott finished the game with a season-best 209 all-purpose yards and three touchdowns as the Cowboys rallied twice in the final 115 seconds to beat their longtime rival. The stars have changed from Staubach to Aikman to Prescott for the Cowboys and instead of Terry Bradshaw throwing deep balls to Lynn Swann, Ben Roethlisberger is throwing them to Antonio Brown.

The rivalry was forged in the 1970s when the finesse Cowboys lost Super Bowls X and XIII to the physical Steelers. Win those games, and the Cowboys are probably the team of the '70s, and players such as Drew Pearson, Cliff Harris, and Harvey Martin are in the Hall of Fame.

The teams met again in Super Bowl XXX, and the Cowboys won 27–17, their unprecedented third Super Bowl championship in four seasons.

They don't play often—only seven times since Jones bought the team in 1989—but their history always seems to make it special. These days, however, the rivalry is a lot more about the fans than the players.

On a perfectly clear, 56-degree, November day, the crowd at Heinz Field roared as Prescott stepped under center from the Dallas 17. A holding penalty on Zack Martin made it first-and-25. A seven-yard completion to Cole Beasley put the Cowboys in the unenviable position of second-and-18 trailing 12–3 with 27 seconds left in the first quarter.

Prescott dropped back and faked a throw right, then he lobbed a pass to Elliott who had three offensive linemen in front of him. Doug Free threw the first block as Elliott cut upfield and received a block from Martin, who bulled a defender into the sideline, and center Travis Frederick took out another as Elliott neared the 40. He made a subtle move to cut inside another defender, and receiver Terrance Williams added a

Ezekiel Elliott celebrates his 32-yard, fourth-quarter touchdown run against the Steelers on November 13, 2016, in Pittsburgh. The last-second score gave the Cowboys a 35–30 victory.

Elliott ran for a season-high 209 yards and three TDs in the Cowboys' come-from-behind win over the Steelers.

couple of blocks as Elliott zoomed down the field and did some kind of leaping dive with a half twist into the end zone to complete the 83-yard scoring play.

In a back-and-forth contest that featured seven lead changes, Elliott had his best game of the season. The screen pass was only the beginning. Elliott used speed, power, athleticism, and vision to frustrate Pittsburgh's defense. He finished with 21 carries for 114 yards, hardly his best overall rushing performance, though he did surpass the 1,000-yard mark. The line played so well that Elliott averaged 3.9 yards per carry before contact, according to ESPN's Stats & Information.

Elliott, though, performed best at winning time, when the Cowboys needed him most and the Steelers knew he'd be getting the ball. Pittsburgh took a 24–23 lead with 7:51 left in the fourth quarter on Le'Veon Bell's one-yard run. If Elliott hadn't been so spectacular, most of the talk following the game would've centered on Bell, who had 134 yards of total offense and two touchdowns.

Prescott and Elliott erased the lead on the next possession. The Cowboys drove 75 yards in 10 plays, converting two third-down plays along the way. A 14-yard pass to Witten on third-and-8 from the Pittsburgh 28 moved the ball to the 14 at the two-minute warning. On the next play, Elliott burst through a large hole off the right side behind a block from Martin and went untouched into the end zone as Dallas took a 29–24 lead after their two-point conversion failed. The touchdown run eliminated any and all discussion about whether the Cowboys should have held the ball longer or if Elliott should've slid at the 1 to set up a field goal as time expired to keep the ball away from Roethlisberger.

Well, Roethlisberger took the Steelers 75 yards in just five plays, throwing a 15-yard touchdown pass to Antonio Brown on a fake spike. Pittsburgh's two-point-conversion attempt failed for the fourth time during the game, and Pittsburgh led 30–29 with 42 seconds left.

"I looked at him before the drive and said, 'Dak, this is why we're here. This is why we came to Dallas,'" Elliott said during an on-field interview after the game. "He didn't flinch. We know what we're capable of. We have unbelievable confidence in each other."

Still, they needed to gain at least 40 yards to set up a makeable field-goal attempt by Dan Bailey at one of the league's most difficult venues for kickers. A 10-yard completion to Cole Beasley picked up a first down and moved the ball to the 35, and a 13-yard toss to Witten put the ball at the Dallas 48 with 23 seconds left. A quick out to Witten netted only five yards, but rookie safety Sean Davis accidentally grabbed Witten's face mask as the veteran fought for extra yardage. The penalty moved the ball to to the Pittsburgh 32 with 15 seconds left.

Backup guard Joe Looney reported as a third tight end because the plan was for Elliott to plunge into the line and set up the game-winning attempt by Bailey from no more than 49 yards away.

Instead, Elliott burst through a hole in the left side behind a clearing block from Gavin Escobar, a player stuck on the bench, in part, because he's a poor blocker and there was no one to block him.

The Steelers had sent everyone crashing into the line to stop the play, so there was nothing for Elliott to do but contemplate his celebration on his way into the end zone. "It parted like the Red Sea," Elliott said in the locker room. "All I had to do was run." He held the ball aloft in his right hand as he sprinted into the end zone. "I was just shaking my head like `Wow," Prescott said. "We were just trying to get us in position to get in good field goal range and Zeke said otherwise." ★

Elliott runs for one of his three touchdowns of the game versus the Steelers.

Zeke and Dak

Cowboys' Rookie Stars Became Fast Friends

They kid because they care—and nothing is off-limits, which is the way it is between friends like Dak Prescott and Ezekiel Elliott. That means Prescott's hairline is always fair game—his shoe game too—but that's what friends do. Prescott and Elliott met at the NFL scouting combine two months before the Cowboys drafted them, and they quickly built a relationship because the foundation of each player's success has been hard work. They're grinders, players who take practice as seriously as games because they have a thirst to succeed.

Elliott, a Nike client, even made fun of Prescott's Adidas tennis shoes and posted a couple of videos on Twitter for his more than 1 million followers to see. The friends regularly play "laundry basketball," which became the rage among players last season. Their chemistry—on and off the field—is among the reasons the Cowboys' thrived without Tony Romo. Their relationship ensures the Cowboys don't have any of the ego issues that can crop up between young stars and wreck a franchise as each battles for fame, money, and endorsements.

Prescott is genuinely happy for Elliott's success and publicly praises the running back with regularity. The same goes for Elliott, who speaks glowingly of Prescott whenever the quarterback's name is mentioned. "We're guys that have been hanging out as soon as we got drafted, from the time we showed up for rookie minicamp," Prescott said at his locker. "He's like a brother. We hang out often off the field and a lot in the locker room." They have done national TV interviews together. No jealousy exists. It's about winning.

The better Elliott plays, the easier it makes Prescott's job because play-action passes become more effective, and Elliott can take the ball in short-yardage situations on second and third down that take the pressure off the quarterback. The better Prescott plays, the easier it makes Elliott's job because he faces more defenses designed to stop the pass than the run.

"Just that chemistry, man, the way we communicate, the way we go out there and play for each other," Elliott said. "Whenever one of us is down, we pick each other up and we hold each other accountable. I think that's the most important part—that we can hold each other accountable and we have that mutual respect where no matter what we say to each other, whether it's good or bad, we're going to listen."

Jason Witten understands the relationship Prescott and Elliott have better than most because he had a

Dak Prescott and Ezekiel Elliott celebrate Elliott's touchdown in the Cowboys' 42–21 *Monday Night Football* win against the Detroit Lions on December 26, 2016.

similar relationship with Tony Romo. Theirs is a friendship that began the day each arrived in Dallas and shared a shuttle ride to the club's Valley Ranch training facility. For 14 years they've been friends, teammates, and confidants.

"You get your first check together. You stay at the hotel for an extended period of time. You deal with the grind of being a rookie and having to go do the silly stuff that comes with being a rookie, and then you also set your goals together," Witten said in front of his locker. "And that was something for Tony and me at that time to be able to go through life and chase your dreams, that's a great feeling. For them to be in the backfield like they are and having a chance to play early and having success, it's great to see relationships like that. I think it brings energy to everyone, but you are excited for them to be able to have that and hold each other accountable as their careers take off. That is a great thing for them."

Elliott and Prescott, road-trip roommates, couldn't appear to be more different. Elliott is forever the life of the party, while the bow-tie wearing Prescott comes off as more serious. Each is solely committed to winning, but they spend their free time differently. You're more apt to find Prescott on a boat fishing, while Elliott prefers clubbing no matter what city he's visiting. During the bye week, Prescott returned home to Haughton, Louisiana, to hang out with his grandmother and family, while Elliott took in a game at LSU. "I tried to get Dak to hang out, but he wouldn't return my calls," Elliott said with a smile.

They occasionally party together like when they hung out with guest DJ Snoop Dogg at Punk Society in the Deep Ellum section of Dallas after a September win over San Francisco. Even when they're not hanging together, they have the same tastes. After a win over

Prescott hands off to Elliott in a game against the Tampa Bay Buccaneers.

Cincinnati, they each dined at Plano's Del Frisco Grill with family to celebrate the victory.

And then there were the Christmas gifts Elliott bought for Prescott and himself—14K white gold pendants covered in diamonds from IF & Co. in Los Angeles. Each piece has both players' jersey numbers (21 and 4), which just happens to be the Dallas area code. The website TMZ.com reported the pieces cost at least $10,000. In Elliott's pendant the 21 is highlighted in blue stones and outlined in diamonds; in Prescott's pendant the 4 is highlighted in blue stones and outlined with diamonds. Elliott wore his to the Cowboys December 26 game against the Detroit Lions. After the 42–21 win, he jokingly searched Prescott's duffel bag while he dressed, searching for the pendant so he could persuade the quarterback to wear it to his postgame news conference. A laughing Prescott declined, but promised to wear it soon. It's a little gaudy for Prescott's tastes, but he didn't want to hurt Elliott's feelings.

That's what friends do. ★

A fan (above) holds aloft a "Prelliott" banner at AT&T Stadium in Arlington, Texas, during a game against Philadelphia. Prescott and Elliott (right) during a game at home against the Washington Redskins.

Dez and Dak

The Rookie QB and His Veteran, All-Pro Receiver

The story, which already has become part of Dallas Cowboys lore, occurred on a practice field at the Cowboys' Valley Ranch training complex. It was the instant when the relationship between Dak Prescott and Dez Bryant was forged and the moment the Cowboys knew Prescott had the intangibles needed to replace Tony Romo as the starter for as long as he was needed.

The Cowboys were going through a two-minute drill when Bryant caught a pass and made a move to get additional yardage instead of going out of bounds and setting up a field-goal attempt. Prescott acted instinctively, sprinting to Bryant and delivering a stern message face mask to face mask. "You are the baddest man on the field, the best player on the team," Prescott told Bryant, according to Bleacher Report. "But you have to listen to me. I told you that you had to get down. Look what just happened. We have the best kicker in the league."

Bryant replied, "I got you, man. It won't happen again."

As the quarterback and de facto leader of the offense, it was Prescott's job to confront Bryant, who could either accept or reject the quarterback's message. Reject it, and it could've really ripped the Cowboys apart because Prescott wouldn't have had the freedom to lead. Instead of reacting to situations, he'd be wondering what to do every time he wanted to make a decision. Accept it, and it would give Prescott permission to lead the offense.

That moment set up Prescott for success because it allowed Bryant and the rookie quarterback to develop a connection before the season. It was a connection that prompted Bryant to praise the rookie all season to anyone who had time to listen and defend him when he needed it.

So, when Bryant caught just one pass for eight yards in the opener against the Giants in a 20–19 loss, no meltdown happened. That's because of the bond Prescott formed with the wide receiver in training camp. Also, Jason Witten and Cole Beasley had a combined 26 targets and 17 catches. "We'll get him the ball as it comes up in our offense," Prescott said after the game. "We're not gonna single out and say Dez has to get the ball on this play."

And when Prescott had consecutive subpar performances against Minnesota and the New York Giants on consecutive weeks in December, Bryant's support for Prescott never wavered. "I'm talking to the fake Cowboy fans. I'm talking to the bandwagoners.

Dak Prescott celebrates with Cowboys wide receiver Dez Bryant after hooking up for a touchdown against the Baltimore Ravens in a 27–17 Dallas win on November 20, 2016.

In a *Sunday Night Football* game against the Bears on September 25, 2016, Prescott hits Bryant in stride (above) for a 17-yard touchdown in the fourth quarter. Prescott greets Bryant in the end zone afterward (right), and the Cowboys sailed to a 31–17 victory.

I'm talking about everybody. Just, first off, just jump off. Jump off," Bryant said, standing at his locker after a win over Tampa Bay. "We lost one game, we was 11–2. Like, come on, man. This guy put us in this position, and you just get to talking crazy. We have one bad game. It's crazy. This is why everybody gets blocked out. We gotta stick together. We've gotta just focus on ourselves and keep on pushing and not pay attention to the noise like the fake praise. We've gotta treat the fake praise like the haters. All the same."

There was no greater example of the depth of the relationship between Prescott and Bryant than when the quarterback helped Bryant work through his father's death. Bryant had a complicated relationship with his father, MacArthur Hatton, who had impregnated Bryant's mother when she was 15. Bryant learned of his father's death the day before the Steelers' game. Prescott, who had lost his mother to cancer as a sophomore at Mississippi State, sent his teammate a heartfelt text. Bryant kept the text, according to Bleacher Report, which read:

Dez, I heard about your loss. I want to let you know I've been through it. First and foremost, I want to let you know nobody, I mean nobody, can tell you how you are supposed to feel. There

aren't any words to comfort someone except he is in a better place than this world, and there is not anything to say to make you feel better right now. Please know I'm here for you, brother. I love you, man, and anytime you want to talk about this or anything, my ears are open. I know I'm young, but I've been through damn near everything, so I don't hesitate. Today is your day. This game is the only thing that gives me peace. That's why I'm so passionate about it, and I know you are the exact same way. Let's go have a day and honor your dad.

Bryant caught six passes for a season-high 116 yards—his third 100-yard game of the season—and a critical touchdown in the Cowboys' thrilling 35–30 win. On third-and-11 from midfield late in the third quarter, Prescott slid left to avoid pressure from a blitzing linebacker and launched a deep ball down the left sideline that Bryant caught at the 5 and sprinted into the end zone, giving Dallas a 23–18 lead.

"We kind of shared this morning about the things I have been through," Prescott said. "I kind of let him know this game brings you peace and use it that way. Your father, he is watching you. He's got the best seat in the house, and I told him to go out there and honor him today, and Dez did exactly that."

After the touchdown, instead of throwing up the X, his signature touchdown celebration, Bryant patted his heart twice with his left hand and thrust his right index finger into the air. Prescott, pointing toward the heavens, sprinted the length of the field to celebrate in the end zone, where Bryant was on one knee surrounded by teammates. After the game, coach Jason Garrett presented Bryant with a game ball.

"They're more like brothers—family, if you will—than teammates. Dez is one of the most relationship-oriented people I've ever met," Garrett said. "That's why he's so beloved by his teammates. Everybody loves Dez. They love what he's all about. They love his passion for the game. They love his passion for the team. They love his passion for the relationships he has within the team. People would run through the wall for Dez Bryant. Anybody who has been around him would do that because they know he'd do the same for them."

And the game, as it does for a lot of players, helped take Bryant's mind off his grief. The field served as his sanctuary. "I'm going to say something that he may not say," Jerry Jones said in the locker room. "If he would want to be any place in the world after finding out he just lost his daddy, he would want to be around these people in this locker room and their love."

Despite the circumstances, Bryant said he felt unusually calm throughout the day and the game. "Usually for games I'm pumped, I'm amped, I have a million things running through my head," Bryant said a few days after the game at his locker. "That Pittsburgh game…I never felt that way ever before. I was calm. I played my best football. I ran the best routes I ever ran with the Cowboys. A lot of credit goes to Dak." ★

Bryant hauls in a 50-yard touchdown pass (left) from Prescott at the end of the third quarter to put the Cowboys up 23–18 over the Steelers in a game Dallas eventually won 35–30 in Pittsburgh. Bryant and Prescott (above) at a practice in Frisco, Texas, on October 26, 2016.

Romo's Speech and Dak's Team

The changes were subtle, virtually imperceptible early in the season as Dak Prescott sought his place in the Cowboys locker room. They grew more noticeable as the Cowboys piled up wins and Prescott became more confident and secure with his role on the team.

Prescott's natural inclination is to lead, but he also wanted to be respectful to Tony Romo, who was expected to miss the first half of the season after suffering a compression fracture in his back in the third preseason game. After all, Romo had started 127 regular-season games since 2006 and played in four Pro Bowls, and when he was ready to return to the lineup, Prescott would go to the bench and watch a maestro do his thing.

So Prescott made a point to be deferential to Romo. A day after leading the Cowboys to a come-from-behind road win over the Washington Redskins, Prescott attended an NFL Play 60 outing with the rest of his rookie teammates. "This is Tony's team," he said. "I knew that going into the situation. I think everybody knew that. I'm just trying to do the best I can to give my team a chance to win week in and week out."

No one disputed that. On his weekly radio show, owner Jerry Jones praised Prescott but made it clear he believed Romo gave the Cowboys their best chance for success. After Prescott led the Cowboys to four consecutive wins, Jones' sentiment had not changed. "Tony would be the first to tell you it's everybody's team, but still, it's Tony's team," Jones said on 105.3 The Fan. "Tony has the experience, and he has the ability to make us a better team. That's the only way you look at it right now."

Wins over Chicago, San Francisco, and Cincinnati did little to change Prescott's mindset. The Cowboys were 4–1 and leading the NFC East, but he was still saying all of the right things about keeping the Cowboys in contention until Romo returned. "This is Tony's team," said Prescott, though he indicated for the first time that he'd like to keep playing, if possible. "It's definitely not a distraction to me. That's not my call. It doesn't have anything to do with me. My job is to come in here, like I say, give these guys a chance to win, get better each and every day at practice, and that's all I focus on."

Three more wins over Green Bay, Philadelphia, and Cleveland, and Prescott's tone had definitely changed. Beating the Packers at Lambeau Field and overcoming three poor quarters to lift the Cowboys to an overtime win over the Eagles had clearly buoyed his confidence. Before the game against Philadelphia, *Sunday Night Football* host Mike Tirico said on air that Jerry Jones

Dak Prescott warms up with a pass as he talks with the injured Tony Romo before a game against the Philadelphia Eagles on October 30, 2016, in Arlington, Texas.

had told him, "When you have a hot hand, you have to ride it."

By the time he had passed for 247 yards in a 35–10 blowout win over Cleveland, Prescott was conceding nothing as Romo started getting closer to playing. Every day, players were asked publicly and privately about the prospects of a quarterback controversy. They were asked to compare and contrast the players.

Romo had thrown a few passes in practice during the bye week before the win over Philadelphia. Romo returned to practice, running the scout team, the week of the Pittsburgh game. "We can't control what's going on outside this building," Dez Bryant said at his locker. "Everybody wants to talk. Everybody wants to do all that, say crazy stuff, but, you know, people need to understand those are people just talking. If you're not

Romo watches from the sideline (left) during a game against the Pittsburgh Steelers. Prescott calls the play at the line of scrimmage (above) in the same game.

"He's earned the right to be our quarterback. As hard as that is for me to say, he's earned that right." —Tony Romo

hearing that from Coach Garrett or Mr. Jones or people around this building, it does not matter."

Prescott, based on his earlier answers, could be described as defiant. The Cowboys had won seven straight games, and he had completed 66.5 percent of his passes for 2,020 yards with 12 touchdowns, two interceptions, and a passer rating of 104.2.

Prescott no longer wondered if he could play at this level, he knew it. "They'll make that decision regardless of how my play is if they want to make that," Prescott said in front of his locker. "It's hard for me to say it's Tony's team, my team, or anybody's team. It's a true team, and everybody's playing their part in it."

With Romo as his backup for the first time all season, Prescott threw for 319 yards and two touchdowns as Dallas beat Pittsburgh 35–30. Afterward, the owner made it clear he wasn't changing quarterbacks. "We are going to let the decision make itself," Jones told reporters after the game. "Dak has got a hot hand, and we're going to go with it. It must not be obvious, because I get asked about it every time I open my mouth. It's not hard. It's not hard at all. Tony would make the same decision. That's what you do."

Romo fought for his job. The week before the Pittsburgh win, he lobbied for an opportunity to compete for the starting job. He also traveled to the game on Jones' private plane, where he discussed his role and his future with the owner. Two days later, he read an emotional six-minute statement. He did not take questions. Nor did he inform coach Jason Garrett of his plans. Halfway through the statement, Romo said Prescott deserved to start.

"You see, football is a meritocracy. You aren't handed anything. You earn everything every single day, over and over again. You have to prove it. That's the way that the NFL, that's the way that football works," Romo said. "A great example of this is Dak Prescott and what he's done. He's earned the right to be our quarterback. As hard as that is for me to say, he's earned that right. He's guided our team to an 8–1 record, and that's hard to do. If you think for a second that I don't want to be out there, then you've probably never felt the pure ecstasy of competing and winning. That hasn't left me. In fact it may burn more now than ever."

Romo's statement received praise from most, skepticism from others. Those who liked it called it selfless. Critics wondered why he read a statement instead of speaking from the heart.

"I think that was more for y'all than for me or for this team," Prescott said a day later. "We know each other, how we feel about the situation. He's been a great leader, a great model for me to look up to and watch every day. So I'm not surprised. This is our team. I said that two minutes ago and I'll say it again. Everybody plays a part in our success in what's happened, and they'll play a part in the adversity that comes."

That signified quite a change from Prescott's position in September. ★

Prescott and Romo (above right) talk on the sideline in the first half of a game against the Baltimore Ravens. Romo fist-bumps Prescott (lower right) before the Cowboys' divisional playoff against the Green Bay Packers on January 15, 2017, in Arlington.

Zeke's Kettle Jump

Elliott Breaks Dorsett's Rookie TD Record and Has a Little Fun for a Good Cause

Ezekiel Elliott hurdled five or six defenders during his rookie season, but it was his leap into a Salvation Army kettle that was the enduring image of his rookie year. Elliott slithered off left guard behind blocks from guard Ron Leary and center Travis Frederick and stumbled into the end zone against Tampa Bay as the Cowboys took a 10–3 second-quarter lead. He regained his balance and headed for one of the large red Salvation Army buckets anchored about five yards behind each end zone. Then he hopped into the bucket and squatted down for a couple of seconds. Then he slowly rose and peeked out of the bucket right into the eyes of fullback Keith Smith. Frederick and tight end Gavin Escobar greeted Elliott as he hopped out of the bucket and headed toward the sideline, the ball still tucked in his right hand.

The touchdown broke Tony Dorsett's 39-year-old team record for most touchdown runs by a rookie in franchise history. On the sideline, Dak Prescott joked about the celebration. "I didn't know that you would come creeping out like that. You killed me with that. I didn't know it was that deep."

Elliott, sitting on the bench, while looking at a replay of his celebration, said, "I had to, it was classy. Y'all saved the ball for me, right?" The officials convened, and the Cowboys received a 15-yard unsportsmanlike conduct penalty, which exposed him to a fine from the NFL. The Cowboys' front office didn't seem too bothered by the penalty, considering the celebration was shown on the video board that stretches 60 yards before the ensuing kickoff.

After the game, coach Jason Garrett didn't mind the celebration itself, but warned Elliott not to do it again because the 15-yard penalty could've been costly. "Well, he shouldn't have done it. I thought it was creative, but he shouldn't have done it," Garrett said. "You know that's how the league is going to rule on those things. You have to understand what's legal and what's not legal. You can jump into the stands in Green Bay, but you can't jump into a Salvation Army bucket in Dallas. You've got to be careful about snow angels. All of these different things that we do. So we have to be more mindful of that. I've got to coach that better."

Cowboys owner Jerry Jones also seemed fine with Elliott's celebration. "I think the Salvation Army should give him the highest award," Jones said after the game. "My dream would be for the NFL to really fine me a lot of money, and I'll take them to the Supreme

Ezekiel Elliott peeks out from inside the Salvation Army kettle behind the end zone after scoring a touchdown against the Tampa Bay Buccaneers and celebrating by jumping into it on December 18, 2016.

Court and we'll get the Salvation Army more attention than anybody can get them. What you saw Zeke do is something in his own way, he has that kind of energy. He's like a young puppy. He's like that around the team, and everyone just loves the way he has a zest for life. He really keeps it interesting. You've got to have some of that in a rough, physical environment."

After the game, Elliott revealed more about the kettle jump. In warm-ups, Elliott noticed the kettles in the end zone, and that gave him the idea. He even checked the kettle's depth to make sure there would be no catastrophic consequences if he jumped into the kettle. And just like that, his celebration joined Emmitt Smith's midfield stare against San Francisco in 2000 and Terrell Owens' popcorn celebration in 2007 as the most memorable in franchise history.

"[Coach Jason Garrett] wasn't happy about it with the penalty for special teams," Elliott said. "He or the special-teams coach wasn't happy, so I can't keep making them mad. But, I mean, it's just sitting there right in the end zone, you know. It's the perfect celebration. They're one of our biggest partners, so I had to show them a little bit of love."

Did he ever.

The Jones family has had a long association with the Salvation Army. The halftime show every Thanksgiving Day at AT&T Stadium was created by Charlotte Jones Anderson, Cowboys executive vice president/chief brand officer, when former NBC executive Dick Ebersol asked her to take over the program designed to create awareness and raise money for the organization.

Elliott's 10-second celebration was worth about $4 million in free advertising according to ESPN business reporter Darren Rovell. "We've seen an $80,000 increase in digital donations since the touchdown versus this time last week," Salvation Army Lt. Col. Ron

Elliott hurdles over Buccaneers free safety Bradley McDougald on his way to 159 yards on the day and a 26–20 Cowboys win.

Elliott scores (above) on a two-yard touchdown run to break Tony Dorsett's 39-year-old Cowboys rookie rushing TD record. After the touchdown, Elliott put his unique spin on the celebration by hopping in and crouching down inside the Salvation Army's red kettle (right). The stunt drew a 15-yard penalty for excessive celebration but also spiked donations to the charity.

Busroe told CNBC. And many of the donations, as you might imagine, came in $21 increments.

And in a Monday tweet, NFL spokesman Brian McCarthy said Elliott would not be fined. Common sense had prevailed even though Elliott had said he'd match any fine he received with a donation to the Salvation Army.

FanPrint, an apparel company, created T-shirts and sweatshirts, licensed by the Cowboys and NFL Players Association, and 100 percent of proceeds from the "Zeke Kettle Leap" apparel went toward Salvation Army, according to ESPN's Darren Rovell.

Anderson said the Cowboys weren't expecting such an amazing response in the 48 hours following the kettle jump. "People are captivated," Anderson said on KTCK 1310-AM in Dallas. "They want to do more and want to jump on to continue the momentum, and this just happened to be momentum for a great cause. I think [Zeke] recognized that and realized, 'Wow, I can do something really special here—let's keep going.'"

Elliott certainly wasn't trying to create a controversy, and with the NFL relaxing the rules on celebration in 2017, he could make the kettle jump an annual December celebration. "When we go out there, we have fun, but we get to work, and I think we're at our best when we're having fun," Elliott said. "Having fun is key." ★

Green Bay

A Tough Playoff Loss to an Old Rival

Emmitt Smith will tell you the game he remembers more than any other in his illustrious career is the Dallas Cowboys' 38–28 loss to San Francisco in the 1994 NFC Championship Game. Troy Aikman feels the same.

The Cowboys trailed 21–0 six minutes into the first quarter, but pulled to within 10 points in the fourth quarter. If a controversial non-call for pass interference against Deion Sanders, who was covering Michael Irvin, had gone the Cowboys' way, they would've had first-and-goal at the 1 with half of the fourth quarter left, and a comeback would've been a real possibility. To Smith and Aikman, that game encapsulates everything the Cowboys of the '90s were all about: heart and mental toughness.

Perhaps one day Dak Prescott and Ezekiel Elliott will look back at their 34–31 NFC divisional playoff loss to the Green Bay Packers at AT&T Stadium the same way Aikman and Smith view that 1994 loss.

The Cowboys won 13 games and finished with home-field advantage throughout the playoffs for the first time since 2007—former coach Wade Phillips' first season—when they lost in the divisional round to the New York Giants, who eventually won the Super Bowl. Tony Romo led that team. While his controversial weekend trip to Cabo San Lucas during the bye week before the game didn't affect his preparation or performance, it created a perception that Romo spent the rest of his career fighting.

Prescott, viewed as one of the team's hardest workers, spent the season evolving into the leader of these Cowboys, while Elliott was always the epicenter of the offense. They spent the season taking the pressure off the defense by finishing second in the NFL in time of possession, while consistently giving them leads to protect. In 2016 the Cowboys ran just 37 of 1,058 plays while trailing by more than a touchdown.

Dallas, a four-point favorite, took an early 3–0 lead over Green Bay, but three possessions into their first playoff game, Prescott, Elliott, and the Cowboys trailed 21–3—their largest deficit of the season—after the defense allowed scoring drives of 75, 90, and 80 yards. It would've been easy to panic and yield to frustration. After all, the Packers had won seven consecutive games and bore no resemblance to the team the Cowboys had overwhelmed 30–16 in October.

That Aaron Rodgers was struggling. This Aaron Rodgers was in the zone. In his last three games, he had passed for 1,009 yards and 12 touchdowns. The Packers

Ezekiel Elliott takes a handoff from Dak Prescott in the Cowboys' divisional playoff game versus the Green Bay Packers on January 15, 2017.

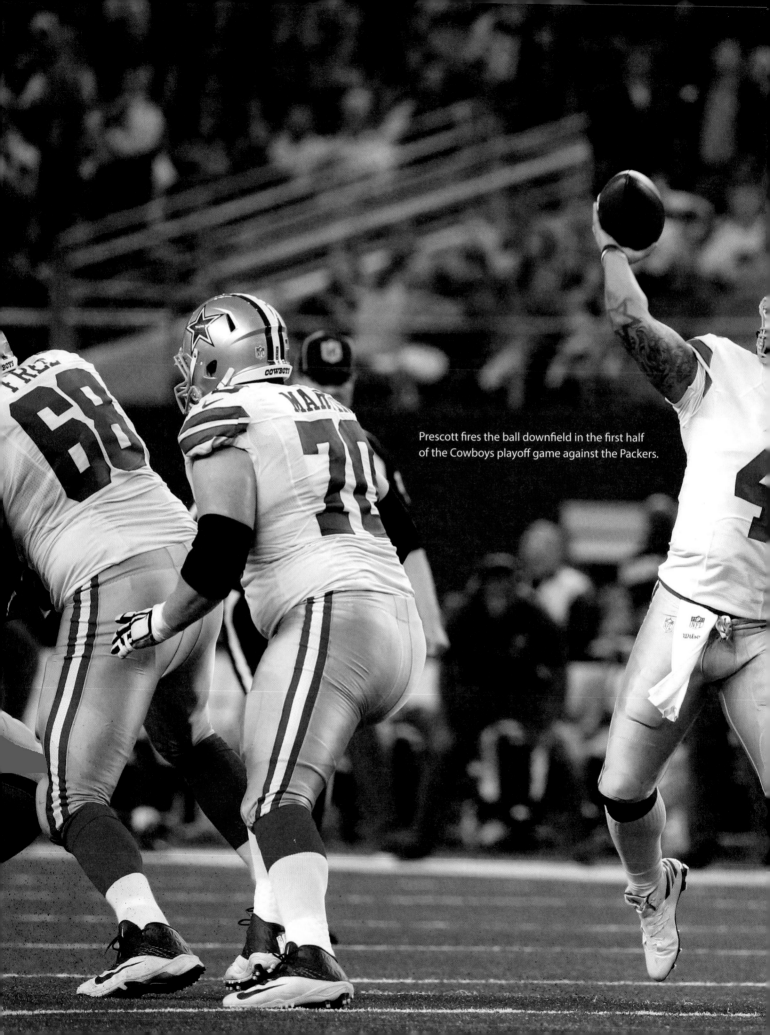

Prescott fires the ball downfield in the first half of the Cowboys playoff game against the Packers.

had hammered the New York Giants and their vaunted defense 38–13 in their NFC wild-card game.

Instead of panicking, Prescott and Elliott went to work. A 40-yard touchdown pass to Dez Bryant made it 21–10, and a 33-yard field goal by Bailey with 1:03 left in the first half trimmed the Packers' lead to 21–13 at halftime. Prescott finished the first half 10-of-18 for 147 yards, while Elliott had 10 carries for 44, but no run longer than nine yards.

Green Bay took the second-half kickoff and drove 75 yards in six plays for a 28–13 lead it would take into

the fourth quarter. But Prescott, who engineered five fourth-quarter comebacks and had a 106.4 fourth-quarter passer rating with six touchdowns and no interceptions, often played his best football with the game on the line.

Prescott completed 13 of 17 passes for 142 yards, two touchdowns, and a two-point conversion in the Cowboys' final three possessions.

A seven-yard touchdown pass on a slant to Dez Bryant pulled the Cowboys to within two at 28–26. Prescott converted the two-point conversion on a

Prescott tries to get a pass off before being brought down by Packers linebacker Nick Perry in the second half. The Cowboys trailed throughout the divisional playoff, but Prescott managed to lead his team to tie the game twice in the fourth quarter at 28–28 and 31–31 before falling to Green Bay in the end, 34–31.

quarterback draw. He ran over 240-pound linebacker Jake Ryan at the Green Bay 1 and spun into 324-pound defensive lineman Kenny Clark, as his churning legs carried him over the goal line, tying the score at 28–28.

A 56-yard field goal by Mason Crosby gave Green Bay a 31–28 lead with 1:33 left.

"We were really rolling in the fourth quarter," Elliott said after the game. "We were going to do anything to win that ballgame. We looked at each other before the drive happened and talked about scoring and said, 'This is where the great ones are made.' We handled our business and we did it."

Completions of 24 yards to Terrance Williams, 11 yards to Witten, and seven yards to Cole Beasley set up Bailey's game-tying 52-yard field goal with 35 seconds left.

That was too much time for Rodgers. On third-and-20 from the Green Bay 32, Rodgers rolled left and completed the kind of pass only a future Hall of Famer can complete to tight end Jared Cook, who made a sliding catch for 35 yards along the left sideline. Officials reviewed the catch and upheld the play. Then Crosby kicked the game-winner as time expired from 51 yards away. As Green Bay's players jubilantly streamed onto the field, an anguished Prescott bent over at the waist, hands on his knees.

Prescott finished with 302 yards passing, becoming the first rookie in the Super Bowl era to throw three touchdown passes in a playoff game. Elliott, the league's leading rusher, finished with 125 yards. "It was a missed opportunity," Prescott said after the game. "This team won't be back together, not the same team, not the same exact men and players won't be back together. But for the people who will for this organization, the youth in this team, it's a building block. We're going to get better from it. We'll make plenty more runs."

Still, it was another season that ended in profound disappointment for owner Jerry Jones. The Cowboys have not been to the NFC Championship Game since the 1995 season, also the last time they played in a Super Bowl. Only the Washington Redskins and Detroit Lions (1991) have a longer drought. The Cowboys have two playoff wins in the last 21 seasons.

"There's no moral victory here," Jones told reporters after the loss. "There might have been a moral victory if we had continued to play the way it was looking earlier, but for this bunch to come back, get it together, and to see those guys come back and compete like that, then I know if we won this game we were capable of doing a good job against, in this case, Atlanta and probably a good job in the Super Bowl." ★

Prescott walks off the field after the Cowboys were eliminated from the divisional round of the 2016 playoffs by the Packers.

Pro Bowl

When the 2016 season began, no one would've been surprised if Ezekiel Elliott earned a trip to the Pro Bowl. The Cowboys took him with the fourth pick of the draft, gave him a terrific offensive line, and had a coaching staff committed to running the ball. Dak Prescott had a much different story. His rookie year was supposed to be a developmental season as the third quarterback behind Tony Romo and Kellen Moore.

Well, the beauty of sports is that it's the world's best reality show. No one ever sees the script before it plays out, and time after time what we anticipate happening doesn't occur. There's no better example than the 2016 Dallas Cowboys, who used the rookie combination of Elliott and Prescott to win 13 games for the third time in franchise history in a highly entertaining manner. Their reward: Elliott and Prescott ranked 1–2 in Pro Bowl voting, which meant they started the game. Kansas City kick returner Tyreek Hill was the only other rookie to earn a trip to the Pro Bowl, which was played in Orlando, Florida, the week before the Super Bowl.

Left tackle Tyron Smith, center Travis Frederick, and guard Zack Martin were also voted to the Pro Bowl. Oakland (seven) and Atlanta (six) were the only teams with more players voted into the game than the Cowboys. The rosters were determined by using the votes of fans, players, and coaches. Each group accounted for a third of the voting.

Prescott, who set club rookie records in passing yards, touchdowns, attempts, completions, and wins, became the first rookie quarterback in franchise history to be selected to the Pro Bowl.

"It's actually a great experience once you're there," coach Jason Garrett said. "In some ways, it's a dubious distinction. You don't want to be the team coaching in the Pro Bowl because it means you've lost in this round."

The Pro Bowl is never about the game, unless the players give so little effort that commissioner Roger Goodell feels compelled to wonder publicly how to make the game more competitive. For Prescott, the week leading up to the game was about hanging around one of the quarterbacks he idolized as a kid in Haughton, Louisiana. "To be the starting quarterback over Drew Brees? Come on, let's be serious. It's definitely humbling," Prescott told reporters. "He is one the greats. He is one of my favorites in everything he does. He is so detailed. We are out at the Pro Bowl. He is still hitting every drill, throwing every ball. One speed. It's the right way to do it. I learned a lot for him."

The 38-year-old Brees, playing in his 10th Pro Bowl, said Prescott impressed him during the season. "Not only did he play with a lot of confidence, but I think he allowed everyone around him to play with a lot of confidence," Brees told dallascowboys.com. "He helped create that. He's a cool customer. He's got a presence

The Cowboys' rookie backfield duo of Dak Prescott and Ezekiel Elliott in action at the Pro Bowl on January 29, 2017, in Orlando, Florida. Ranked 1–2 in the Pro Bowl fan voting, Prescott and Elliott started the game, the only rookies to do so.

Elliott, as you can imagine, used the week to have as much fun as he could.

about him that's hard to explain. It's a confidence, but also you can tell he's got leadership ability."

Elliott, as you can imagine, used the week to have as much fun as he could, especially during the skills challenge the day before the game. He enjoyed a wild shirtless celebration after helping his team win the dodgeball competition, and he even tried to get some practice time at defensive end after switching jerseys with Seattle defensive end Michael Bennett when he wasn't lobbying for a chance to attempt a field goal. "I've done nothing but have fun," Elliott said of the week. "It's great vibes out here. We have a tremendous amount of respect for each other. We all respect each other's games. We're spending time and learning from each other but having fun at the same time."

The actual Pro Bowl game was largely uneventful for Elliott—at least on the field—and Prescott as the AFC beat the NFC 20–13. Elliott rushed eight times for 20 yards and contributed a tackle on punt coverage that probably stopped Tyreek Hill from scoring after a 38-yard return down the right sideline. Prescott completed seven of 13 passes for 52 yards, and Dez Bryant caught five passes for 59 yards.

Elliott, however, was involved in the game's most notorious moment.

Prescott, Dez Bryant, and Elliott pose for a selfie (left) at NFC practice in Florida a few days before the Pro Bowl. Elliott (above) runs upfield with a smile at practice the next day.

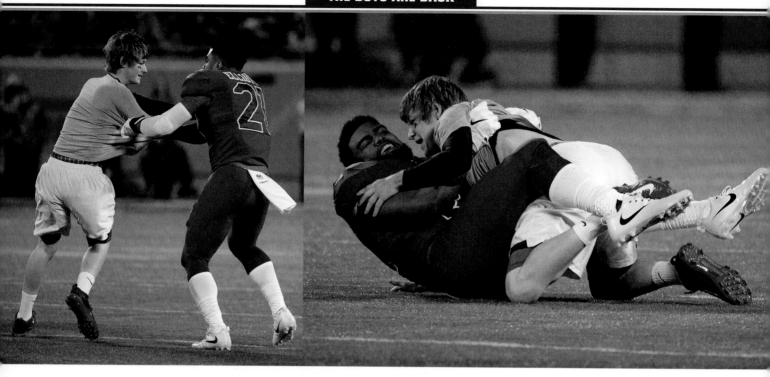

A fan ran out of the stands and onto the field and Elliott chased him. An AFC defensive lineman put the fan in a bear hug, but then let him go and the fan started sprinting toward the end zone. Elliott sprinted alongside him. As the fan, wearing a Superman T-shirt, entered the end zone, he imitated Cam Newton's "Superman" touchdown celebration wearing a Superman shirt. Then security, with an assist from Elliott, walked him off the field.

The week, no matter how much they enjoyed it, didn't erase the sting from losing to Green Bay. They would rather have been preparing for the Super Bowl instead of a game that didn't count in the standings. "It's behind me, but I can't say I'm over that loss," Prescott told reporters after Wednesday's Pro Bowl practice. "I'll never be over that loss. I'll never be over any loss. It's definitely fuel to the fire and [I'm]

ready to get back to work. As much as this is a great experience, obviously, I would have wanted to play next week [in the Super Bowl]. But this is the next-best thing."

Elliott had a similar sentiment. But it's also important for each of them not to let the disappointment of their playoff loss affect their memory of a successful season. Elliott led the NFL in rushing and carries and could've had a chance to break Eric Dickerson's rookie rushing record of 1,808 yards if he hadn't sat out the season's last six quarters.

"Sometimes, I gotta step back and look and see what I did and appreciate it," Elliott said. "I have such high expectations. I think about the season, and I wanted to be in the Super Bowl, but I gotta realize what I've done and the honors I've received and know how special it is. I'm definitely not satisfied." ★

Elliott made the most of his Pro Bowl experience—enjoying practice with Prescott before the game (right) and taking down a fan who ran onto the field during the game (above).

No Sophomore Slump

In the months after his first NFL season ended, Dak Prescott signed endorsement deals with Tostitos, Pepsi, and Nicholas Air, a company with a fleet of private planes. As the 135th pick in the draft, he signed a four-year contract worth $2.7 million, which is about eight times less than Ezekiel Elliott earned in 2016. So Prescott's taking advantage of the opportunities afforded him as the Cowboys' quarterback was understandable, but also raised the question of whether he would lose any focus or if his thirst for success would be quenched.

Well, most of those questions were answered during the Cowboys first off-season OTA when he proclaimed himself bigger, faster, and stronger than he was as a rookie based on his results from the off-season conditioning program, which measures growth in categories such as 20-yard dash, bench press, vertical jump, and flexibility. Prescott putting in the off-season work to improve physically should help him avoid the dreaded sophomore jinx so many folks talk about.

The same goes for Elliott, who rushed for 1,631 yards and 15 touchdowns as a rookie. The offensive line lost left guard Ron Leary, who signed a four-year, $35 million deal with Denver, and right tackle Doug Free, who retired after starting 114 games in his nine-year career. The Cowboys expect to replace Leary with Jonathan Cooper, a former first-round pick, who was a bust after being taken seventh overall by Arizona in 2014. La'el Collins, who started three games at guard before a toe injury ended his season, is expected to replace Free at tackle.

Defensive coordinators will study Elliott and attempt to take away his best plays, but as long as the offensive line jells and play-caller Scott Linehan continues to make Elliott the epicenter of the offense, it's going to be hard to stop him.

Besides, running backs, unlike other positions, typically enter the NFL in their prime. Their production reduces dramatically the closer they get to 28, while other positions tend to enter their athletic prime from about 28–30, when their mental understanding of the game and their physical prowess are each at an apex.

Running backs tend to have their production dip dramatically after they turn 28 because, even though they still have enough speed and quickness to get to the hole, they've lost the ability to accelerate through it.

Many of the NFL's best running backs are usually more effective in their second season. Adrian Peterson rushed for 1,341 yards as a rookie and 1,760 in his second year. Eric Dickerson made history in his first two years, setting the NFL rookie rushing record with 1,808 yards and topping it with a league-record 2,105 yards in Year 2. Each of those records still stands.

Emmitt Smith gained a league-leading 1,563 yards in his second season after picking up 937 as a rookie. It

Now entering their second year as starters, quarterback Dak Prescott and running back Ezekiel Elliott practice the exchange during OTAs at the Cowboys training facility in Frisco, Texas, in May 2017.

Prescott putting in the off-season work to improve physically should help him avoid the dreaded sophomore jinx.

was the first of three straight rushing titles for the NFL's all-time leading rusher.

"I'm working on becoming a more dominant second-level runner," Elliott said. "I think there were a couple of times last year when I could've been better on certain runs. So I'm just kinda focused on finishing my runs and making guys miss at the second level."

If he can do that, Elliott will be an even bigger threat. He led the league with 48 runs of 10 yards or more, five more than Chicago's Jordan Howard. He also led the NFL with 14 runs of 20 yards or more, three more than Buffalo's LeSean McCoy.

When folks talk about Prescott regressing in Year 2, the conversation usually revolves around the rapid descent of 2012 Rookie of the Year Robert Griffin III or Nick Foles, who threw 27 touchdown passes and just two interceptions in 2013. Each played in a gimmick offense; Prescott did not.

Griffin rushed for 815 yards on 120 carries yards as Mike Shanahan exploited NFL defenses unfamiliar with stopping the zone read. When injuries forced him to become a pocket passer to thrive, he couldn't do it.

Foles played in Philadelphia coach Chip Kelly's gimmick offense that fooled defensive coordinators for a year, which is why Foles had the NFL's third-best touchdown/interception differential in 2013 (which he did it in just 10 games) behind Denver's Peyton Manning and New Orleans' Drew Brees. He's had 23 touchdowns and 20 interceptions since then, while becoming a backup.

Prescott, 6'2" and 226 pounds, has a thick frame that allows him to withstand the punishment that accompanies the position. And, when he runs or scrambles, he's quick to slide and avoid big hits. "There's nothing flukey about Dak's game," Cowboys scouting director Will McClay said. "He's just a good quarterback. He doesn't force anything and he makes good decisions."

Defensive coordinators will spend the off-season taking away his favorite throws and plays, forcing Prescott and the coaching staff to adjust. Play-caller Scott Linehan and coach Jason Garrett must continue to be creative, and Prescott must be patient and avoid turnovers.

The notion that he's destined to have a sophomore slump is folly. The Cowboys went all-in with Prescott last season, tangible evidence they believed he could replicate his performance. Prescott's potential is the main reason why Tony Romo became a TV analyst with CBS in April 2017.

Prescott put in a great deal of work in the off-season to make himself bigger, stronger, and faster than he was as a rookie.

"He is trying to get himself ready for every opportunity he has, as quarterback, in the meeting room, walk-through, practice, games, in the weight room," Garrett said. "He is just one of those guys, and he is a great example for a coach to use with the other players on the team. They naturally follow him. They naturally see how he goes about everything, how ready he is for the chances that he does get."

Plus NFL coaches, scouts, and players will tell you that players tend to improve the most between their first and second seasons. Remember, Prescott spent his first OTA with the Cowboys making sure he had mastered taking a snap from center since he spent much of his time at Mississippi State in the shotgun and learning the offense. Now he's getting the majority of snaps in practice, and the offense is tailored for him instead of Romo.

"Mentally, I think as a quarterback and pretty much at every position, the No. 1 way to get better is the number of reps," Prescott said. "Having a good bit of those [reps] this off-season, I think it's going to allow me to get better with my footwork, get better at the reads, get better going through things faster and being more accurate every day. I don't look at what's behind me. I look at where I want to go and what I can do. The only way I know is through hard work, so it's just something that I continue to try to do." ★

Cowboys offensive coordinator Scott Linehan (left) talks to Prescott and Elliott during OTAs in May 2017. Elliott (above) wants to become an even more dominant second-level runner in 2017.